CARDINAL RAFAEL
MERRY DEL VAL

THE CATHOLIC EDUCATION PRESS   Washington, D.C.

CARDINAL RAFAEL MERRY DEL VAL

A Brief Biography

Philippe Roy-Lysencourt   Translated by Mary J. Gillman

Contents

Abbreviations

AAS	*Acta Apostolicae Sedis*
ACDF	Archivio della Congregazione per la Dottrina della Fede
ACS	Archivio Centrale dello Stato
ASCAES	Archivio della Sacra Congregazione degli Affari Ecclesiastici Straordinari
ASS	*Acta Sanctae Sedis*
ASV	Archivio Segreto Vaticano
MEFRIM	Mélanges de l'École française de Rome—Italie et Méditerranée
PCESJ, AMDV	Pontificio Colegio Español de San José, Archivo Merry del Val

CARDINAL RAFAEL MERRY DEL VAL

INTRODUCTION

RAFAEL Cardinal Merry del Val, despite his historical importance, remains neglected by church historians. Indeed, although hagiographical books on him are relatively numerous, there exists no scientific biography, and works devoted to one or another aspect of his life are almost nonexistent.[1] Yet, one needs only consult a work or an article on church history in the first third of the twentieth century to come across his name. He was an omnipresent figure who, through his roles and

---

1. The most important hagiographic works are as follows: Frances Alice Forbes, *Rafael, Cardinal Merry del Val: A Character Sketch* (London: Longmans, Green, 1932); Pio Cenci, *Il cardinale Raffaele Merry del Val* (Rome-Turin: L.I.C.E.–Roberto Berruti, 1933); Vigilio Dalpiaz, *Attraverso una porpora: Il cardinale Merry del Val* (Turin: L.I.C.E., Roberto Berruti, 1935); Viktor von Hettlingen, *Raphael Kardinal Merry del Val: Ein Lebensbild* (Einsiedeln and Cologne: Benziger, 1937); Girolamo Dal-Gal, *Il Cardinale Raffaele Merry de Val: Segretario di Stato del Beato Pio X* (Rome: Edizioni Paoline, 1953); Hary Mitchell, *Le cardinal R. Merry del Val: Secrétaire d'État de Saint Pie X* (Paris: Paris-Livres, 1956); Marie Cecilia Buehrle, *Rafael cardinal Merry del Val* (Milwaukee: Bruce, 1957); José María Javierre, *Merry del Val* (Barcelona: Juan Flors, 1961); and Alberto José González Chaves, *Rafael Merry del Val* (Madrid: San Pablo, 2004). For other works, see the bibliography at the end of this book.

responsibilities, was involved in the majority of the great ecclesiastical events of his era and who, in front of and behind the scenes, played a major role in the Western world. Why does he no longer arouse any interest among historians? There are several reasons: First, the biographical genre has been and remains rather neglected. Cardinal Merry del Val is not the only papal secretary of state whose life has not been chronicled. There are actually very few secretaries of state about whom a biography has been written, although church historians constantly encounter them in their research.[2] Second, the church of which the cardinal was representative is not the one that rules today. Rafael Merry del Val was one of the major actors of a church that was anti-liberal and uncompromising toward the modern world—a view that does not arouse sympathy currently and most certainly contributes to historians' lack of interest in the cardinal.

It must be said that studying such a person is not easy. To begin with, the archives are superabundant and dispersed throughout numerous countries.[3] Then, extensive research and study is required on the several delicate dossiers with which Cardinal Merry de Val was involved. Furthermore, it is necessary to analyze his role as secretary of state with regard to the relationship of the Holy See with France, Spain, Portugal, and Russia. When it comes to Italy, it would be advisable to examine his ac-

2. See the dossier "Les secrétaires d'État du Saint-Siège (1814–1979): Sources et méthodes," *Mélanges de l'École française de Rome: Italie et Méditerranée* (hereafter MEFRIM) 110, no. 2 (1998): 439–686.

3. See the bibliography at the end of this book.

tions in the politics of the Holy See regarding the Italian state and the time of the "Roman question." Under ecclesiastical duties, it is important to research his role in the fight against modernism, in the changes in Catholic Action, and in the reform of the curia. It is also necessary to study his role as secretary of the Holy Office in the different condemnations issued by this congregation—for instance, that of Padre Pio or the Friends of Israel. It is equally necessary to consider his assessment of the Marian apparition at Fatima and of the different mystical phenomena for which he was responsible. Regarding institutional responsibilities, the modifications that he introduced in the functioning of the Holy Office must be analyzed. And then, beyond the political man, beyond the diplomat and administrator, it is indispensable to study the figure of Cardinal Merry del Val as man and as priest, which is all the more important and delicate since a dossier concerning his beatification was introduced in 1953.[4] Finally, one must study his spirituality and his apostolates—for instance, among the youth of the Trastevere neighborhood of Rome and among the Anglicans. These several examples show that there are many tricky points that need study and clarification.

4. Pontificio Colegio Español de San José, Archivo Merry del Val (PCESJ, AMDV), letter from Msgr. Pedro Canisio van Lierde to "Beatissimo Padre" (Vatican City, February 20, 1953). On the beatification process of the cardinal, see José María Muñoz Urbano, "El cardenal Secretario de Estado Rafael Merry del Val y su proceso de beatificación: Historia de su causa; Problemas, investigaciones de archivos y documentación inédita," Ph.D. diss. (Rome: Pontificia Università Gregoriana, 2008).

In this work, we present a concise biography of Cardinal Merry del Val in such a way as to give a panorama of his life. We follow his journey chronologically on a path that summarizes the great steps that punctuate it. First, we describe the period that encompasses his education, his formation, and his first curial responsibilities, from his birth to the year 1903. We then consider the period 1903–14, during which he was secretary of state for Pius X. Finally, we examine the era during which he was secretary of the Holy Office, from 1914 until his death in 1930.

1

RISE OF A FUTURE PRINCE OF THE CHURCH (1865–1903)

C ARDINAL Merry del Val was born into a privileged
life in which he benefited from a thorough education and received a good formation. When he
arrived in Rome to pursue his studies, he was immediately noticed by Leo XIII, who became attached to the young
man and bestowed honors and responsibilities upon
him. This chapter describes the birth and early years of
Rafael, his journey as a seminarian, the Pious Association
of the Sacred Heart of Jesus that he founded in the Roman
quarter of Trastevere when a young priest, and finally, his
first curial duties until his nomination as secretary of the
conclave of 1903.

Birth and Early Years

Rafael Merry del Val was born in London on October 10, 1865, and was baptized the next day.[1] On his paternal side as well as his maternal side, he was descended from noble cosmopolitan families with Spanish and English connections.[2] His father, also named Rafael, was secretary of the Spanish embassy in Paris, and then in London, before becoming the plenipotentiary minister of Spain in Belgium (1876–87), Spanish ambassador to Austria-Hungary (1887–93), and Spanish ambassador to the Holy See (1893–1901).[3] The Merry del Val family, which included five children, followed Rafael's father to his various posts. Thus, the young Rafael resided in England until 1876,[4] then

1. Pontificio Colegio Español de San José, Archivo Merry del Val (PCESJ, AMDV), fol. 7251, "Certified Copy of an Entry of Birth"; fol. 1090–1090 bis, "Copia dell'atto di nascita di Sua Eminenza redatto dal padre Marchese Raffaele Merry del Val."

2. PCESJ, AMDV, fol. 1035, "Algunos modestos apuntes referentes a la familia de Su Eminencia el Cardenal Merry del Val, y a los primeros años de su vida," written by Domingo Merry del Val, brother of the cardinal.

3. "Merry del Val (Rafael)," *Enciclopedia Universal Ilustrada Europeo-Americana*, vol. 34 (Bilbao, Madrid, and Barcelona: Espasa-Calpe, S. A., n.d.), 981; "Merry del Val (Rafael)," *Enciclopedia Universal Ilustrada Europeo-Americana*, vol. 7 (appendix) (Bilbao, Madrid, and Barcelona: Espasa-Calpe, S. A., 1932), 375; Covadonga de Quintana Bermúdez de la Puente, "Merry del Val, Rafael," *Diccionario Biográfico Español*, vol. 34 (Madrid: Real Academia de la Historia, 2009), 776–77 (this volume, by far the most voluminous, contains errors); José Pablo Alzina, *Embajadores de España en Londres: Una Guía de Retratos de la Embajada de España* (Madrid: Ministerio de Asuntos Exteriores, 2001), 284.

4. PCESJ, AMDV, fol.1036, "Algunos modestos apuntes referentes a la

moved to Belgium. During the first year in this country, he was promoted to the College of Notre-Dame de la Paix at Namur.[5] Afterward, until 1883, he studied at Saint Michael's College in Brussels.[6]

Rafael's report cards show that at first he placed among the lowest of his class, but over the course of the year his grades improved, evidence of constant work on his part.[7] At the end of his school years, he was in the first level of his class.[8] He excelled in two areas: declamation and theater.[9] One of his former classmates, the artist Herman Richir, provided the following anecdote:

Here is a recollection that remains of those times when we were together at the College. During the course of the year there was a presentation of the "Memoirs of the Devil" and,— stinging detail—it was the future Cardinal who filled the role of the devil. I remember that very well because, since I was

familia de Su Eminencia el Cardenal Merry del Val, y a los primeros años de su vida," written by Domingo Merry del Val, brother of the cardinal.

5. Archivio Segreto Vaticano (ASV) Segreteria di Stato, Spogli di Cardinali e Officiali di Curia, Rafael Merry del Val, busta 3, fol. 56, "Compte de MM. Merry Del Val: Alphonse, Raphaël et Pedro," Namur, January 11, 1877.

6. ASV, Segreteria di Stato, Spogli di Cardinali e Officiali di Curia, Rafael Merry del Val, busta 3, fol. 58–75; PCESJ, AMDV, fol. 1036, "Algunos modestos apuntes referentes a la familia de Su Eminencia el Cardenal Merry del Val, y a los primeros años de su vida," written by Domingo Merry del Val, brother of the cardinal.

7. ASV, Segreteria di Stato, Spogli di Cardinali e Officiali di Curia, Rafael Merry del Val, busta 3, fol. 80–91.

8. ASV, Segreteria di Stato, Spogli di Cardinali e Officiali di Curia, Rafael Merry del Val, busta 3, fol. 90–91.

9. ASV, Segreteria di Stato, Spogli di Cardinali e Officiali di Curia, Rafael Merry del Val, busta 3, fol. 80–91.

already drawing, I made a sketch of my comrade in his Mephistopheles costume, which, unfortunately, I failed to preserve.[10]

One of his other classmates affirms that he was a "very good actor."[11] The archives show that Rafael manifested exemplary behavior, that he was involved in several pious associations at his school, and that he was an altar boy.[12] His former classmates emphasized that he was a pious child.[13] One of his teachers, Fr. Kieckens, held him in such high esteem that when he published a book of prayers in 1894, he named it *The Rafael of Christian Souls*, using the first name of his former student.[14]

10. PCESJ, AMDV, fol. 1132, "Copy of a letter from a renowned Belgium painter," to Fr. Léon Morel, SJ, Brussels, May 20, 1930. This is a testimony of Mr. Herman Richir (1866–1942), PCESJ, AMDV, fol. 1135, letter from Fr. Léon Morel to Fr. S. Arendt, Brussels, June 11, 1930.

11. PCESJ, AMDV, fol. 1139, extract of a letter from Fr. Milcamps, SJ, to Fr. Léon Morel, SJ, s.l. n.d. For the name of this father, see PCESJ, AMDV, fol. 1136, letter from Fr. Léon Morel to Fr. S. Arendt, Brussels, June 11, 1930.

12. PCESJ, AMDV, fol. 1116, "Notizie del Card. Segret. di Stato Merry del Val, date dal R.P. de Wouters S.I. già direttore del Collegio St. Michel," s.d.

13. For example, PCESJ, AMDV, fol. 1133, "Extract of the Letter from a Distinguished Attorney," to Fr. Léon Morel, SJ, Etterbeek, May 20, 1930, concerning the testimony of Mr. Graind'Orge; PCESJ, AMDV, fol. 1136, letter from Frl. Léon Morel to Fr. S. Arendt, Brussels, June 11, 1930; PCESJ, AMDV, fol. 1133, "Extract of a Letter from a Very Distinguished Person," to Fr. Léon Morel, SJ, concerning the testimony of Mr. Paul De Streel; PCESJ, AMDV, fol. 1136, letter from Fr. Léon Morel to Fr. S. Arendt, Brussels, June 11, 1930; PCESJ, AMDV, fol. 1138, extract of a letter from Fr. Paul Goethals, SJ, to Fr. Léon Morel, SJ, s.l. n.d.

14. J.-F. Kieckens, *Le Raphaël des âmes chrétiennes: Nouveau recueil de prières méditées, de dévotions solides et de pratiques efficaces empruntées aux meilleurs*

The testimonies are unanimous that Rafael was held in high esteem by his teachers and his comrades. One of the Jesuits who taught him wrote, "He is distinguished by a perfect dependability, a fervent piety, and he has gained the affinity of his teachers and his companions."[15] Fr. Renard, supervisor of the boarding students when Rafael entered, described him as being "a pearl in the midst of the students who were not all models of behavior"; one could "say that here was a perfect scholar, full of distinction and piety." Fr. Renard added that "this was the nature of his brothers," who also "had received a quality education," and that "the parents . . . were of a remarkable distinction."[16] Fr. de Wouters did not think any differently. He wrote that the fathers, the superiors, and the teachers found in the distinction and the elevation of affinities of Rafael and his brothers "not only a delightful elegance or a great personal compassion, but a fine example for and a happy influence on their classmates."[17] One other priest, a supervisor at the school during the time when

ascètes de la Compagnie de Jésus (Brussels: Maison Van de Vivere, 1894). PCESJ, AMDV, fol. 1141, extract of a letter from Rev. Fr. Boller, SJ, to Fr. Léon Morel, SJ, s.l. n.d. For the name of this father, see PCESJ AMDV, fol. 1136, letter of Fr. Léon Morel, SJ, to Fr. S. Arendt, Brussels, June 11, 1930.

15. PCESJ, AMDV, fol. 1137, extract of a letter from Rev. Fr. Van Nylen, SJ, to Fr. Léon Morel, SJ, s.l. n.d. For the name of this father, see PCESJ, AMDV, fol. 1136, letter from Fr. Léon Morel to Fr. S. Arendt, Brussels, June 11, 1930.

16. PCESJ, AMDV, fol. 1137, extract of a letter from Rev. Fr. Renard, SJ, to Fr. Léon Morel, s.l. n.d. For the name of this father, see PCESJ, AMDV, fol. 1136, letter from Fr. Léon Morel to Fr. S. Arendt, Brussels, June 11, 1930.

17. PCESJ, AMDV, fol. 1116, "Notizie del Card. Segret. di Stato Merry del Val, date dal R. P. de Wouters S.I. già direttore del Collegio St. Michel," s.l. n.d.

Rafael was there, wrote, "This was a young man of exemplary conduct, of great distinction, and a singular dignity and nobility. He was esteemed by his classmates and his teachers."[18]

Seminarian

In 1883, after his humanities studies, Rafael joined a seminary in northern England, St. Cuthbert's College at Ushaw.[19] He stayed there for two years and received the tonsure and the four minor orders on October 5, 1884[20]— on the same day, as was then customary[21]—from Bishop

18. PCESJ, AMDV, fol. 1141, extract of a letter from Rev. Fr. Boller, SJ, to Fr. Léon Morel, SJ, s.l. n.d. For the name of this father, see PCESJ AMDV, fol. 1136, letter of Fr. Léon Morel, SJ, to Fr. S. Arendt, Brussels, June 11, 1930.

19. Regarding St. Cuthbert's College, see Rev. Henry Gillow, *The Chapels at Ushaw with an Historical Introduction* (Durham, U.K.: George, Neasham, 1885); An Old Alumnus, *Records and Recollections of St. Cuthbert's College, Ushaw; with Introductory Poem, To which are appended copious Illustrative, Historical, and Descriptive Notes* (Preston: E. Buller and Son, 1889); Edwin Bonney, "Ushaw College," in *The Catholic Encyclopedia*, vol. 15 (New York : Robert Appleton, 1912), 233–35; André Leroux, *Enquête sur la formation des clercs à l'étranger: Ushaw College* (Moulins: Crépin-Leblond, 1933); David Milburn, *A History of Ushaw College: A Study of the Origin, Foundation and Development of an English Catholic Seminary with an Epilogue 1908–1962* (Durham, U.K.: Ushaw Bookshop, 1964); William James Campbell, ed., *Ushaw College 1808–2008: A Celebration* (Durham, U.K.: St Cuthbert's Society, 2008).

20. ASV, Segreteria di Stato, Spogli di Cardinali e Officiali di Curia, Rafael Merry del Val, busta 3, fol. 117, testimonial letter dated October 11, 1886, regarding the conferral upon Rafael Merry del Val, on October 5, 1884, of the four minor orders by Mgr John William Bewick, bishop of Hexham and Newcastle.

21. PCESJ, AMDV, fol. 1189, letter from Msgr. William Godfrey (then

Bewick, bishop of Hexham and Newcastle.[22] The archives of the establishment do not provide much information about his brief time there. There are neither notes nor commentaries from his professors; there is not even a course program or any other document that would provide information about the formation he received.[23]

In 1885 he was sent to pursue his studies in Rome. He intended to enter the Pontifical Scottish College, but his plans were disrupted by Leo XIII. Indeed, upon arriving in the Eternal City, he was received with his father at a private audience with the pope. During this interview, Leo XIII commanded the young man to go to the Pontifical Academy of Ecclesiastical Nobles rather than the Scottish College.[24] The young seminarian was at a loss for words and gave in to the order of the supreme pontiff. This audience was the beginning of a dazzling career in the curia for the young Rafael Merry del Val.

The mission of the Academy of Ecclesiastical Nobles was to form young clerics for the diplomatic services of the Holy See and for the administrative service of the curia.[25] This was the front door to a promising career in the

---

the apostolic delegate in Great Britain) to Jaime Flores Martin (rector of the Spanish College), London, August 6, 1953.

22. "Hexham and Newcastle," *Tablet*, October 11, 1884.

23. Ushaw College Library, Merry del Val papers.

24. PCESJ, AMDV, fol. 1036, "Algunos modestos apuntes referentes a la familia de Su Eminencia el Cardenal Merry del Val, y a los primeros años de su vida," written by Domingo Merry del Val, brother of the cardinal.

25. Regarding this institution, see Ferdinando Procaccini di Montescaglioso, *La Pontificia Accademia dei Nobili Ecclesiastici* (Rome: Tip. A. Befani, 1889); *La Pontificia Accademia Ecclesiastica: 1701–1951* (Vatican City, 1951);

service of the Holy See. Rafael Merry del Val entered this institution in 1885 and remained there until 1891 while continuing his studies at the Gregorian,[26] where he obtained a doctorate in philosophy in 1886,[27] a doctorate in theology in 1890,[28] and a license in canon law in 1891.[29] The principal question that must be asked here is why Leo XIII commanded this young man, whom he had just met for the first time, to enter into this institution, when such a request absolutely did not correspond to the wishes of the young seminarian. In the absence of sources that would answer this question with certitude, a historian can only formulate hypotheses. The decision was certainly linked to a convergence of several elements. There are three principal reasons that could explain the pope's order. First, the young man possessed the ideal profile. He

A. Martini, "La diplomazia della Santa Sede e la pontificia Accademia ecclesiastica," *La Civiltà Cattolica* 2 (1951): 372–86; *Regolamento da osservarsi dai Signori Convittori dell'Accademia Ecclesiastica di Roma* (Rome: Stamperia Salomoni, 1802; reprinted in 1982); *Pontificia Accademia Ecclesiastica, Terzo centenario (1701–2001)* (Rome, 2003); Claude Prudhomme, "L'Académie pontificale ecclésiastique et le service du Saint-Siège," *MEFRIM* 116 (2004): 61–89.

26. Archives of the Pontifical Academy of Ecclesiastical Nobles, *Libro segnato B*; Cenci, *Il cardinale Raffaele Merry del Val*.

27. ASV, Segreteria di Stato, Spogli di Cardinali e Officiali di Curia, Rafael Merry del Val, busta 3, fol. 116, certificate of doctorate in philosophy of Rafael Merry del Val, Pontifical Gregorian University, July 18, 1886.

28. ASV, Segreteria di Stato, Spogli di Cardinali e Officiali di Curia, Rafael Merry del Val, busta 3, fol. 138, certificate of doctorate in theology of Rafael Merry del Val, Pontifical Gregorian University, June 30, 1890.

29. ASV, Segreteria di Stato, Spogli di Cardinali e Officiali di Curia, Rafael Merry del Val, busta 3, fol. 145, certificate of license in canon law of Rafael Merry del Val, Pontifical Gregorian University, November 26, 1891.

was the issue of a great family from whom he had received a thorough education. He was multilingual, and his father was a career diplomat. In addition, Leo XIII seems to have liked Rafael the father, who ended his career as the ambassador of Spain to the Holy See. And finally, the pontiff seemed to be attached to the young man and personally took care to confer charges and honors upon him. In June 1887 Leo XIII chose him to be the secretary of the pontifical mission to London to present his felicitations to Queen Victoria during the golden jubilee of her reign.[30] On this occasion, Leo XIII named Rafael Merry del Val secret supernumerary chamberlain.[31] This honorific distinction bestowed on him the title of "Monsignor" while he was still a student and not yet a priest or even a subdeacon. Furthermore, Leo XIII sent his own tailor to take measurements from him for a new habit, illustrating the paternal disposition of the pontiff toward the young cleric.[32]

Several months later, in March 1888, Leo XIII named

30. Archivio della Sacra Congregazione degli Affari Ecclesiastici Straordinari (ASCAES), Inghilterra, 1886–88, pos. 111, fasc. 45, "Istruzioni per Monsig: Ruffo Scilla Incaricato dal S. Padre a complimentare la Regina d'Inghilterra per il 50th anno della sua esaltazione al trono" (London, 1887); ASV, Segreteria di Stato, Spogli di Cardinali e Officiali di Curia, Rafael Merry del Val, busta 3, fol. 120, letter from Cardinal Mariano Rampolla to Rafael Merry del Val (senior) (Rome, June 16, 1887).

31. ASV, Segreteria di Stato, Spogli di Cardinali e Officiali di Curia, Rafael Merry del Val, busta 3, fol. 119, Prefettura dei SS. Palazzi Apostolici, Dalle Stanze al Vaticano, no. 486, June 8, 1887, document signed by Msgr. Luigi Macchi.

32. Cenci, *Il cardinal Raffaele Merry del Val*, 36–37.

Rafael secretary of a pontifical mission to Berlin to represent him on the occasion of the funeral of Emperor Wilhelm I and the coronation of Frederick III.[33] In December 1889, he was once again named secretary of a pontifical mission, this time to the imperial court of Vienna.[34] Meanwhile, he was ordained a subdeacon in Prague on September 29, 1887,[35] deacon in Rome on May 27, 1888,[36] and priest in that city on December 30 of the same year.[37]

The Pious Association of the Sacred Heart of Jesus

Several months after his priestly ordination, the president of the Academy of Ecclesiastic Nobles entrusted to Rafael Merry del Val the task of being the spiritual adviser of the youth of the Mastai pontifical school in the Trastevere, which was run by the Brothers of the Christian Schools.[38] This apostolate was the origin of the Pi-

33. ASCAES, Stati Ecclesiastici, 1887–88, pos. 1083, fasc. 355 (Berlin, 1888).

34. Cenci, *Il cardinal Raffaele Merry del Val*, 37.

35. PCESJ, AMDV, fol. 1191, "Suddiaconato di Sua Eminenza Card. Merry del Val."

36. PCESJ, AMDV, fol. 1175, "Diaconato et presbiterato di Sua Eminenza."

37. ASV, Segreteria di Stato, Spogli di Cardinali e Officiali di Curia, Rafael Merry del Val, busta 3, fol. 126, testimonial letter attesting the priestly ordination of Rafael Merry del Val by Cardinal Lucido Maria Parocchi on December 30, 1888, Rome, January 5, 1889; PCESJ, AMDV, fol. 1175, "Diaconato et presbiterato di Sua Eminenza."

38. Also known as the Christian Brothers or the De La Salle Brothers; F. A.,

ous Association of the Sacred Heart of Jesus, which Rafael founded in 1889.[39] According to the association's rules, its aim was to bring together the best young people from the Christian schools of Trastevere "to preserve and intensify in them the spirit of piety and zeal for their sanctification and that of their companions" in the said association "and to awaken in their hearts, with a lively love towards the heart of Jesus, the ardent desire to make reparation and expiation for the offenses that are made against Him by ungrateful souls." The association had three ends: "(1) To render unto Jesus love for love. (2) To imitate the virtues taught and practiced by the Divine Master during His mortal life. (3) To make reparation and expiation by every possible means for the sins of man and especially for those committed against the Blessed Sacrament."[40]

Rafael Merry del Val was not satisfied with supervising things from afar. He was actively involved in this association until the end of his life, as Cardinal Nicola Canali testified:

He assembled all the youth in the chapel for exercises of piety. He heard their confessions, taught them the fundamental principles of the faith and Christian morals, inculcated in

---

"Sua Eminenza e l'Associazione," *Caritas: Bollettino mensile dalla Pia Associazione del S. Cuore di Gesù in Trastevere*, no. spécial "Sua Eminenza Reverendissima Il Signor Cardinale Raffaele Merry del Val," s.d., 3.

39. PCESJ, AMDV, fol. 470, *Pia Associazione del Sacro Cuore de Gesù fondata nel 1889 nelle Scuole Cristiane in Trastevere: Ricordo dell'anno 1911.*

40. PCESJ, AMDV, *Regole della Pia Associazione de Sacro Cuore de Gesù eretta nelle Scuole Cristiane de Trastevere nel 1989* (Rome: Tipo Litografia Consorti, 1903), 5.

them a holy fear of God, and a devotion to the Blessed Virgin Mary, especially during the month of May. In order to keep an eye on them, he took part in their recreations and their games, and sometimes he himself took them to the Pontifical Sanctuary of the Holy Stairs (the Scala Sancta) or to the catacombs. He also took them on an annual excursion to the Castelli Romani area where he had them visit several sanctuaries. All this took place over the course of forty consecutive years.[41]

First Curial Duties

After his priestly ordination, Rafael Merry del Val continued his ascent in the curia. On December 31, 1891, Leo XIII took him directly into his own service by naming him a secret chamberlain.[42] In June 1893, he was sent to Austria-Hungary to present the red biretta to Cardinal Lörinc Schlauch, bishop of Oradea Mare in Romania.[43]

Two-and-a-half years later, in December 1895, Leo XIII named him deputy secretary of the special Pontifical

41. *Vaticana Beatificationis et Canonizationis Servi Dei Raphaëlis Card. Merry del Val Secretarii Status Sancti Pii Papae X: Summarium Super Dubio An signanda sit Commissio introductionis Causae in casu et ad effectum de quo agitur* (1957), 291, testimony of Cardinal Nicola Canali.

42. ASV, Segreteria di Stato, Spogli di Cardinali e Officiali di Curia, Rafael Merry del Val, busta 3, fol. 146, certificate of nomination of Rafael Merry del Val as a secret chamberlain, signed by Cardinal Mariano Rampolla del Tindaro, secretary of state, December 31, 1891.

43. PCESJ, AMDV, fol. 1202; *Beatificazione e canonizzazione del servo di Dio il cardinale Raffaele Merry del Val, Segretario di Stato del beato Pio X: Articoli per il processo ordinario informativo* (Tipografia Poliglotta Vaticana, 1952) 6.

Commission for the Union of Dissident Churches.[44] The following year, he was named secretary of the Pontifical Commission to examine the question of the validity of Anglican ordinations.[45] It was not without reason that Leo XIII put Rafael Merry del Val to work on Anglican questions. Indeed, the young priest was directly concerned with the conversion of Anglicans. His great hope was to be able to consecrate his life to their conversion, and he was already carrying out an apostolate toward them in Rome.[46] Starting in 1898, under the order of the pope, he collaborated in the refounding of the Pontifical Beda College, a seminary intended to form and prepare for the priesthood converts from Anglicanism who aspired to return to England to exercise their ministry.[47] In addition,

44. ASV, Segreteria di Stato, Spogli di Cardinali e Officiali di Curia, Rafael Merry del Val, busta 3, fol. 213, certificate of nomination of Rafael Merry del Val as adjunct secretary of the Pontifical Commission for the reunion of dissident churches, secretary of state, December 9, 1895.

45. Archivio della Congregazione per la Dottrina della Fede (ACDF), *Sanctum Officium, De Ordinibus Sacris*, 1897, no. 1, *Della Consecrazione episcopale e delle sacre Ordinazioni presso gli Anglicani* I. Regarding the subject of this commission and Rafael Merry del Val's work, see *La validité des ordinations anglicanes: Les documents de la commission préparatoire à la lettre "Apostolicae Curae,"* vol. 1, *Les dossiers précédents*, introduction, transcription, and notes by André F. von Gunten, OP, with the collaboration of Msgr. Alejandro Cifres, Fontes Archivi Sancti Officii Romani 1 (Firenze: Leo S. Olschki Editore, 1997); *La validez de las ordenaciones anglicanas: Los documentos de la comisión preparatoria de la bula "Apostolicæ Curae,"* vol. 2, *Los documentos de 1896*, introducción, transcripción y notas de Mons. Alejandro Cifres, Fontes Archivi Sancti Officii Romani 2 (Rome: Libreria Editrice Vaticana), 2012.

46. Cenci, *Il cardinal Raffaele Merry del Val*, 42–45.

47. PCESJ, AMDV, fol. 2846–57, Anonymous, "A Brief sketch of the History of the College of Venerable Bede in Rome," s.l., n.d.

he was involved in the Opera della preservazione della fede,[48] founded in 1898 at the behest of Leo XIII, "to promote those works which most directly oppose Protestant propaganda."[49] Regarding this subject, it should be mentioned that in 1904 he published a book titled *The Truth of Papal Claims* to defend the rights of the pope against the Protestants.[50] He had personally converted to Catholicism many Protestants whom he himself had abjured and whom he continued to encourage thereafter.[51]

In March 1897, his career took a new leap forward when he was named the apostolic representative to an extraordinary mission to Canada[52] and prelate of His Holiness.[53] The goal of his mission was "to work toward

48. Cenci, *Il cardinal Raffaele Merry del Val*, 44–45.

49. ASV, Segreteria di Stato, 1909, r. 66, fasc. unico, *Opera della Preservazione della Fede sotto la protezione di Maria SS.ma Immacolata e dei principi degli apostoli S. Pietro e S. Paolo*, Tipografia Poliglotta della Congregazione De Propaganda Fide, May 1901; cited in Raffaella Perin, "L'atteggiamento della Chiesa cattolica verso ebrei e protestanti da Pio X a Pio XI," doctoral thesis in historical sciences (Università degli Studi di Padova, 2010), 39.

50. Raphael Merry del Val, *The Truth of Papal Claims: A Reply to "The Validity of Papal Claims" by F. Nutcombe Oxenham, D.D. English Chaplain in Rome* (London: Sands; St. Louis: B. Herder, 1904), xvi, 129, xv.

51. *Vaticana Beatificationis et Canonizationis Servi Dei Raphaëlis Card. Merry del Val... Summarium Super Dubio An signanda sit Commissio introductionis Causæ in casu et ad effectum de quo agitur* (1957), 293–95, testimony of Cardinal Nicola Canali.

52. ASV, Segreteria di Stato, Spogli di Cardinali e Officiali di Curia, Rafael Merry del Val, busta 3, fol. 214, notice of the appoint of Rafael Merry del Val as apostolic delegate to Canada, March 10, 1897.

53. ASV, Segreteria di Stato, Spogli di Cardinali e Officiali di Curia, Rafael Merry del Val, busta 3, fol. 216, brief of the nomination of Rafael Merry del Val as domestic prelate of His Holiness, Rome, March 13, 1897.

easing tensions and facilitating the return of a friendly working relationship between the episcopate and the Canadian government, by means of a good settlement of the educational question of Manitoba."[54] Specifically, the Holy See asked him to apply himself to bring together the bishops and the government, to sound out the disposition of the latter so as to ameliorate the conditions of the Manitoba Catholic schools, to verify whether it would be possible to obtain a satisfactory solution to this question, to make sure that the instructions of the Holy See regarding the political election be observed exactly, and last, to inquire about the state of ecclesiastical matters in Canada and refer to the Holy See everything he considered as meriting attention.[55]

The mixed success of his mission and the displeasure of several Canadian bishops did not stop his ascent in the curia.[56] In July 1898, he was named consultor to the Sa-

54. ASCAES, Session 807, October 17, 1897, Stampa 586, 1, Sacra Congregazione Degli Affari Ecclesiastici Straordinarii, *Canadà, Questione scolastica ed ingerenza del clero nella politica*, *Ponenza*, September 1897, letter from Cardinal Mariano Rampolla del Tindaro to Wilfrid Laurier, Rome, March 14, 1897.

55. ASCAES, Session 807, October 17, 1897, Stampa 586, 1, *Canadà, Questione scolastica ed ingerenza del clero nella politica*, *Ponenza*, 31–32, *Istruzioni date a Monsig: Delegato Apostolico al Canadà* (March 9, 1897).

56. ASCAES, Session 783, February 11, 1897; Session 796, June 21, 1897; Session 807, October 14, 1897; Session 809, December 11, 1897; Session 825, July 11, 1898; ASCAES, Inghilterra, 1897, Posizione 161, fasc. 90–103, Canada, 897; Inghilterra, 1897–1898, Posizione 162, fasc. 104, Canada *Québec–Montréal*–1897; Inghilterra, 1897–1898, Posizione 163, fasc. 104–5, Canada, 1897–1898.

cred Congregation of the Index.[57] The following year, in October 1899, Leo XIII placed him at the head of the Pontifical Academy of Ecclesiastic Nobles.[58] Several months later, on May 6, 1900, he was consecrated titular archbishop of Nice.[59]

At the Pontifical Academy of Ecclesiastic Nobles, Rafael, at the request of Leo XIII and Cardinal Rampolla, reformed the formation of future diplomats of the Holy See.[60] At the time of his appointment as the head of this institution, on June 12, 1900, a new rule of studies was approved.[61]

During this period, Leo XIII continued to entrust him with missions. On June 3, 1902, he was named as the representative of the pope to the coronation of King Ed-

57. ACDF, Archivum Indicis Librorum Prohibitorum, Diarium 22, *Acta Sacrae Indicis Congregationis*, 1894–1907, fol. 38r, July 6, 1898.

58. ASV, Segreteria di Stato, Spogli di Cardinali e Officiali di Curia, Rafael Merry del Val, busta 3, fol. 230, notice of the appointment of Rafael Merry del Val as president of the Pontifical Academy of Ecclestiastic Nobles, Segreteria di Stato, October 23, 1899.

59. ASV, Segreteria di Stato, Spogli di Cardinali e Officiali di Curia, Rafael Merry del Val, busta 3, fol. 233, notice of the appointment of Rafael Merry del Val as titular archbishop of Nice, signed by Cardinal Mariano Rampolla del Tindaro, secretary of state, April 5, 1900.

60. ASCAES, Italia, 1900, Posizione 640, fasc. 214, Rome—1900, letter from Mgr Rafael Merry del Val to Cardinal Mariano Rampolla del Tindaro, s.l., March 6, 1900.

61. ASCAES, Stati Ecclesiastici, 1900, Posizione 1232, fasc. 391, *Roma—1900, Regolamento per gli studii speciali della Pontificia Accademia de' Nobili Ecclesiastici*. ASCAES, Italia, 1900, Posizione 640, fasc. 214, *Roma—1900, Programma degli studi ai quali devono applicarsi i signori dell'Accademia de' Nobili Ecclesiastici secondo le prescrizioni emanate dalla Santità di Nostro Signore Leone Papa XIII nel 1900*, (Rome: Tipografia Artigianelli di S. Giuseppe, 1900).

ward VII of England.[62] Several months later, on November 30, 1902, he became adviser to the Commission for the l'Opera della preservazione della fede.[63]

The death of Leo XIII on July 20, 1903, was the occasion of Archbishop Merry del Val's new assignment, which subsequently determined the rest of his career. The Sacred College at that time found itself in difficulty, since Msgr. Alessandro Volpini, secretary of the Sacred College, had died unexpectedly several days before the pope and there was no one to prepare, organize, and conduct the conclave. It was necessary to find a successor quickly, and it was Archbishop Merry del Val who was chosen.[64]

62. ASV, Segreteria di Stato, Spogli di Cardinali e Officiali di Curia, Rafael Merry del Val, busta 3, fol. 264, notice of the appointment of Rafael Merry del Val as pontifical representative to the coronation of King Edward VII of England, Segreteria di Stato, June 3, 1902.

63. ASV, Segreteria di Stato, Spogli di Cardinali e Officiali di Curia, Rafael Merry del Val, busta 3, fol. 265, notice of the appointment of Rafael Merry del Val as member of the Consulta Prelatizia della Commissione Cardinalizia per l'Opera della preservazione della fede, Segreteria di Stato, November 30, 1902.

64. ASV, Segreteria di Stato, Morte di Pontefici e Conclavi, Pio X, Scatola 14/B, fasc. 9, fol. 5.

2

SECRETARY OF STATE FOR PIUS X (1903–1914)

A T THE END of the conclave that elected the successor of Leo XIII, the new pope named Rafael Merry del Val pro-secretary of state, a position that Merry del Val held until his appointment as secretary of state. In this chapter, we consider the reasons behind these appointments and the life of the prelate at the side of Pius X.

Pro-Secretary of State

After the death of Leo XIII, Guiseppe Sarto was elected pope on August 4, 1903.[1] The same day, although he had

1. Archivio Segreto Vaticano (ASV), Segreteria di Stato, Morte di Pontefici e Conclavi, Pio X, Scatola 14/B, fasc. 9.

only met Merry del Val the first time several days before and had not spoken to him for more than several minutes, he named the young Msgr. Rafael Merry del Val pro-secretary of state.[2]

How can this extraordinary appointment be explained? It can only be understood if the circumstances of the situation are made clear. During the night of the election, around 8:30 p.m., Msgr. Merry del Val, secretary of the conclave, went to Pius X's chamber to have the pope sign the letters to the heads of state officially announcing his election, and then, as his work was finished, to take his leave. But, according to Cardinal Merry del Val, Pius X said to him, "Monsignor, do you want to abandon me? No, no, remain, remain with me. I have not yet made a decision; I do not know what I want to do. For the moment, I have no one, so stay with me as pro-secretary of state . . . then, we will see. Do this for me as a friend."[3] So the first reason seems to be that Pius X, who came from Venice and who had no curial experience, found himself a little destitute. He did not know the men in the central administration of the Vatican and did not know from among whom to make his choices, notably for the central post of secretary of state. He needed some time to think. On the other hand, he had an immediate need for someone, since he did not know the workings of the Vatican machine very well. But why did his choice stop with this

2. Merry del Val, *Pie X: Impressions et souvenirs* (St-Maurice: Éditions de l'Oeuvre de St-Augustin, 1951), 26–27.

3. Merry del Val, *Pie X*, 26.

young ecclesiastic, who was not even forty years old and whom he did not know? Probably because he appreciated his work as secretary of the conclave. He had had occasion to see the young archbishop at work over a period of several days and had been able to assess his qualities. The evening of August 4, he said to Merry del Val, "I have seen over these days how you have given yourself with enthusiasm to your work."[4] Did someone advise him? Did someone say something good to him about the young prelate during the conclave? This is a possibility. Men speak, but the archives do not contain all that they say. In the absence of additional documentation, we have to stick with that as the explanation of this appointment.

For two and a half months, while waiting for the new pope to name a permanent secretary of state, Rafael Merry del Val supported Pius X as pro-secretary of state. And then, on October 18, 1903, at the end of his daily audience with the pope, the latter gave a large envelope to him, saying, "Oh! Monsignor, this is for you." Since this was not the first time Pius X had done such a thing, Msgr. Merry del Val took the envelope and answered, "Very well, Holy Father, I will look at it and will discuss it with you tomorrow."[5] The envelope contained a signed letter from the pope that said:

The wishes of the Cardinal Eminences who elected you secretary of the conclave, the courtesy with which you have accept-

4. Merry del Val, *Pie X*, 25.
5. Merry del Val, *Pie X*, 38–39.

ed until now to undertake the work of secretary of state, and the so laudable zeal with which you have acquitted yourself in this sensitive office create for me a moral obligation to ask you to assume permanently the position of secretary of state.

For this reason and also to satisfy a heart-felt need to give you a small token of my deep gratitude, at the next consistory it will give me great joy to make you a cardinal of the Holy Roman Church.

I can assure you, for your great consolation, that such an act will be appreciated by the majority of the cardinal eminences who, with me, admire the superior gifts with which the Savior has enriched you and who certainly will permit you to render your best service to the Church.[6]

The envelope also contained a sizable sum of bank notes. In his memoirs of Pius X, the cardinal wrote, "His Holiness, in his paternal goodness, wanted to give me this gift because until then I had not received honorariums, and also because he wanted to contribute to the expenses occasioned by my promotion."[7]

After having read the letter, Msgr. Merry del Val immediately went to see Pius X to dissuade him from making him secretary of state. He noted that Pius X "admitted no attempt to discuss his decision" and said that Merry del Val should "accept the will of God, as he had done so himself in bowing down under the weight of the papacy."[8]

6. Archivio della Sacra Congregazione degli Affari Ecclesiastici Straordinari (ASCAES), Stati Ecclesiastici, 1903–4, Posizione 1267, fasc. 429 (Rome, 1903–12); Merry del Val, *Pie X*, 41–42.

7. Merry del Val, *Pie X*, 40–41.

8. Merry del Val, *Pie X*, 42.

Rafael Merry del Val was the first to be surprised by his appointment. He wrote that Pius X had never revealed to him "even the least little indication of his thinking" about the subject of the appointment of the future secretary of state and that it seemed evident to him that the pope was not thinking of him.[9] Further, this was a position he had never sought and did not want. He wrote, "The heavy burden of the daily occupations did not leave me time to think of other things and I only had one desire: to be free of the heavy responsibility of a temporary position, which no one with any sense would want to see prolonged."[10] Several weeks after his appointment as pro-secretary, on August 23, 1903, he wrote to a religious, "I am very occupied for the moment and I will be so until the Holy Father decides to name a cardinal secretary of state. I hope this appointment will happen soon and I will be able to leave and resume my former occupation."[11] But then, why did Pius X appoint him? Here are the reasons the pope gave to a cardinal:

I chose him because he is a polyglot: born in England, educated in Belgium, of Spanish nationality, and living in Italy; the son of a diplomat and himself a diplomat, he is familiar with the problems of all countries. He is very modest. He is a saint. He comes here every morning and informs me of all the

9. Merry del Val, *Pie X*, 37–38.
10. Merry del Val, *Pie X*, 38.
11. Pontificio Colegio Espanol de San José, Archivo Merry del Val (PCESJ, AMDV), copy of a letter from Rafael Merry del Val to Fr. Lacoste, Vatican, August 23, 1903.

problems of the world. I need never make an observation to him, and he never compromises principle.[12]

Cardinal and Secretary of State

Rafael Merry del Val was created cardinal by Pius X in a private consistory on November 9, 1903,[13] and received the red hat two days later, on November 11.[14] That day, after the speech given by the new cardinal,[15] the pope told him:

> Lord Cardinal, the good odor of Christ that you have diffused everywhere ... and the many works of charity to which you have dedicated yourself continuously in your priestly ministry, especially in this city of ours, with admiration, have gained you universal esteem, which we believe you have been able to deduce for yourself ... from the sincere demonstrations that have been made for you on these occasions.[16]

The next day, November 12, Cardinal Merry del Val was named a member of the Sacred Congregation of the Roman and Universal Inquisition and of the Congregations of the Council, of Rites, and of Extraordinary Ecclesias-

12. Pio Cenci, *Il cardinale Raffaele Merry del Val* (Rome and Turin: L.I.C.E.– Roberto Berruti, 1933), 138.

13. *Acta Sanctae Sedis (ASS)* 36 (1903–4): 193–98, 276.

14. ASV, Segreteria di Stato, Spogli di Cardinali e Officiali di Curia, Rafael Merry del Val, busta 4, fol. 272, bull by which Pius X conferred the presbyterial title of St. Praxedes to Cardinal Rafael Merry del Val; *ASS* 36 (1903–4), 278.

15. *ASS* 36 (1903–4): 279–80.

16. *ASS* 36 (1903–4): 280.

tical Affairs.[17] The same year, he was also named prefect of the Laurentana Congregation,[18] president of the Pontifical Commission for Administration of Wealth of Holy See,[19] and member of the Cardinals' Commission for the Preservation of the Faith in Rome.[20]

Rafael Merry del Val was the first cardinal created by Pius X. This position gave him the privilege each year of celebrating Mass in the Sistine Chapel on the occasion of the anniversary of the coronation of the sovereign pontiff. Later, after the death of Pius X and throughout the pontificate of Benedict XV, it was he who came back to celebrate the pontifical Mass when the pope held chapel in the Sistine Chapel on the occasion of the anniversary of the death of his predecessor.[21]

In October 1909, Cardinal Merry del Val became a member of the Congregation of the Consistory.[22] Later, on January 12, 1914, Pius X named him archpriest of St. Peter's Basilica and prefect for the Congregation for the Fabric of St. Peter's, replacing Cardinal Rampolla, who had died the previous month.[23] Numerous witnesses have stated that he exercised great diligence at ceremonies and demanded the same regularity from the canons.[24] In addition, during his sixteen years as head

17. *ASS* 36 (1903–4): 283.

18. *La Gerarchia Cattolica* (Rome: Tipografia Vaticana, 1904), 103–4.

19. *La Gerarchia Cattolica* (1904), 103–4.

20. *La Gerarchia Cattolica* (1904), 480.

21. Cenci, *Il cardinale Raffaele Merry del Val*, 144–45.

22. *La Gerarchia Cattolica* (Rome: Tipografia Vaticana, 1910), 91, 429.

23. *Acta Apostolicae Sedis* (*AAS*) 6, no. 1 (January 19, 1914): 22.

24. Cenci, *Il cardinale Raffaele Merry del Val*, 256–57.

of the basilica, he started several works. Notably, he restored the five organs in the basilica, made a new edition
of the *Officium Maioris Hebdomadae*, restored the tombs
of several popes, and had the length of certain cathedrals
etched into the marble pavement, notably those of Malines, Westminster, St. Paul's of London, and Reims.[25]

It is interesting to compare Cardinal Merry del Val's
term as the head of the Office of Secretary of State with
other persons who have held these duties during modern times. From 1789 to today, there have been thirty-six
secretaries of state. Their average age at the time of their
nomination was sixty. Rafael was appointed at thirty-
eight. Therefore, his age was exceptional, even taking
into consideration that there were other secretaries of
state who were appointed at a young age—for instance,
Cardinal Consalvi, who was first appointed when he was
forty-three. Be that as it may, Cardinal Merry del Val to
this day remains the youngest secretary of state in the
history of the contemporary Curia.[26] It should also be
noted that Rafael Merry del Val was the first non-Italian
secretary of state. After him, there was not another non-
Italian secretary of state until Cardinal Villot was named
in 1969. Another interesting aspect to consider is the
synchronism between the mandate of the secretary of
state and the papacy of which it was a part. This was clear
in the case of Rafael Merry del Val. He was named at the

25. Cenci, *Il cardinale Raffaele Merry del Val*, 258–306.
26. Calculations in part from the site http://catholic-hierarchy.org, as
of April 8, 2015.

beginning of the pontificate of Pius X and was not renewed in the position under Benedict XV. His correspondence with the papal office was so intertwined that history and historians are not able to disassociate the names of
Pius X and Cardinal Merry del Val. It was a unique situation; no other secretary of state's term corresponds so exactly and exclusively with a papacy: either the other popes
had several secretaries of state or the secretaries filled
the position for more than one pope.[27] Consequently, the
appointment of Rafael Merry del Val was atypical because
of his young age, his geographical origin, and the exact
synchrony of his mandate with the papacy of the man who
appointed him.

The Relationship between Pius X
and Rafael Merry del Val

It has been suggested that Cardinal Merry del Val, "in
a certain way, imposed himself on the simplicity of the
pope." It can also be affirmed that "the young, vigorous
and energetic, hard-working secretary of state" had "a
special influence on the Holy Father who, … because of
his rural origins, his rare visits to the Roman Curia, and
his remoteness from political affairs, could not help but
entrust himself entirely to the experience of his secre-

27. Calculations in part from the site http://catholic-hierarchy.org, as of
April 8, 2015.

tary of state."[28] What was really going on? What do the archives show? What was the work relationship and the personal relationship between Pius X and Cardinal Merry del Val?

What the documentation brings out is that the pope truly was in charge, and his secretary of state was the servant of his master. Cardinal Merry del Val was the faithful echo of the doctrine and sentiments of Pius X. Whether it was a matter concerning relations with the Italian state or with foreign states, or it was an internal question of the church, what the archives contain are words like, "The Holy Father gave me an order to announce that ...,"[29] or, "The Cardinal Secretary of State, R. Merry del Val, by order of the Holy Father, asks ...,"[30] or even, "The Holy Father ... is pleased to order that no later than 15 February next, the undersigned Cardinal Secretary of State be given a complete and detailed list."[31] The sources prove irrefutably that Cardinal Merry del Val was an executor of

28. Sacra Rituum Congregatione, *Romana beatificationis et canonizationis Servi Dei Raphaëlis Card. Merry del Val Secretarii Status Sancti Pii Papae X: Animadversiones promotoris generalis fidei super dubio an signanda sit commission introductionis causae in casu et ad effectum de quo agitur* (Typis Polyglottis Vaticanis, 1959), 11–12.

29. Cited in Cenci, *Il cardinale Raffaele Merry del Val*, 160, letter from Cardinal Merry del Val to Msgr. Domenico Accica, September 7, 1903.

30. ASCAES, Stati Ecclesiastici, 1903–4, Posizione 1268, fasc. 429 (Rome 1904), letter from Cardinal Rafael Merry del Val to the secretary of the Sacred Congregation for Extraordinary Ecclesiastical Affairs, s.l.

31. ASCAES, Stati Ecclesiastici, 1903–4, Posizione 1268, fasc. 429 (Rome 1904), letter from Cardinal Merry del Val to the secretary of the Sacred Congregation for Extraordinary Ecclesiastical Affairs, January 21, 1904.

the thought and will of Pius X. Was he always in agreement with him? The archives do not allow an answer of any certainty to this question, but neither do they exhibit any hint of the least disagreement. Pio Cenci, the premier biographer of the cardinal,[32] confirms the following: "People close to the two are in the position to confirm that between the pope and the cardinal secretary of state, during the long period of 11 years, not only was there no disagreement or the least misunderstanding, but the most complete harmony, characterized by an understood cordiality and, one could say, a genuine friendship."[33]

In addition, Rafael Merry del Val had boundless admiration for Pius X. His book *Pie X, Impressions et souvenirs*, is full of this sentiment. Rafael Merry del Val esteemed Pius X for "his humility,"[34] "his inexhaustible charity," "his spirit of sacrifice," and "his ardent zeal for the salvation of souls."[35] He lent "his paternal compassion to all the suffering and all the distress that he discovered, his generous aid of clear counsel, ... his lavish material assistance so overwhelming and with so much sensitivity in public and in private."[36] He also admired in the sov-

---

32. Actually, the work was compiled by Cardinal Canali: *Vaticana beatificationis et canonizationis Servi Dei Raphaëlis Card. Merry del Val . . . : Summarium super dubio . . .* (1957), 265–66, testimony of Cardinal Nicola Canali. Cardinal Canali was assisted with the editing by Giuseppe de Mori. Pio Cenci lent his name and helped with the revision of the proofs.

33. Cenci, *Il cardinale Raffaele Merry del Val*, 239.

34. Merry del Val, *Pie X*, 95–100.

35. Merry del Val, *Pie X*, 43.

36. Merry del Val, *Pie X*, 44.

ereign pontiff "a strength of invincible character," "the most complete mastery [he had] over himself," as well as "a power of will which can be verified by those who lived with him and who were especially struck by it since they had habitually witnessed his constant gentleness."[37]

The devotion of the cardinal toward Pius X did not stop with the death of the latter. After the pope's death on August 20, 1914,[38] Cardinal Merry del Val worked to erect a monument to Pius X in St. Peter's Basilica.[39] At its inauguration on Thursday, June 28, 1923, he delivered a vibrant discourse of devotion and homage to the memory of the pope.[40] Moreover, he went on pilgrimage four times, in 1924, 1925, 1926, and 1929, to the places where Giuseppe Sarto was born and lived.[41] And from the pope's death until the end of his own life, on the 20th of each month the cardinal celebrated a private Mass for Pius X.[42] Further, in his private apartment there were numerous mementos of the pope.[43]

For his part, Pius X took the measure of Cardinal Mer-

37. Merry del Val, *Pie X*.

38. *AAS*, year 6, vol. 6, no. 12 (August 20, 1914): 405.

39. Cenci, *Il cardinale Raffaele Merry del Val*, 297–305.

40. PCESJ, AMDV, fol. 2232–40, *Discorso di Sua Eminenza Revma Il Cardinale R. Merry del Val per la solenne inaugurazione del monumento al papa Pio X nella Patriarcale Basilica Vaticana alla presenza di Sua Santità Pio XI e del Sacro Collegio il 28 giugno 1923* (Rome: Tipografia Poliglotta Vaticana, 1923); *Corriere d'Italia*, Friday, June 29, 1923.

41. PCESJ, AMDV, fol. 5753, "Cardinale Raffaele Merry del Val e la sua villeggiatura in ARABBA."

42. Cenci, *Il cardinale Raffaele Merry del Val*, 375.

43. Cenci, *Il cardinale Raffaele Merry del Val*, 383.

ry del Val's dedication and did not hesitate to point it out. For example, he wrote to him on August 11, 1904, one year after his election:

> I cannot … express to you all my gratitude for your generous marks of affection given to the point of sacrifice, of which I have superabundant and continuous proof from the first days of August of the past year until the present; and I pray that the Lord, as long as it pleases Him to leave me here, gives me the grace to have you always beside me.[44]

Moreover, Pius X worried about the health of his secretary of state, because he was always absorbed in work. During the summer of 1904, he insisted that the cardinal take several days off. On this occasion, he asked Edmondo Puccinelli, the master of the house of the Sacred Apostolic Palace, to set up some rooms in the pontifical apartment at Castel Gandolfo for the cardinal. The cardinal bowed to the insistence of the pope and stayed there for several weeks during the months of August and September. These stays were repeated during the following three years. Edmondo Puccinelli reported that the pope ordered him to prepare the cardinal's quarters carefully and to provide any services he had need of without telling the cardinal, because he would not have accepted them. For the first few years, the cardinal went to Castel Gandolfo by train. The sovereign pontiff then asked Msgr. Pescini, his private chaplain, to accompany the cardinal

44. ASCAES, Stati Ecclesiastici, 1903–4, Posizione 1267, fasc. 429 (Rome 1903–12), letter from Pius X to Cardinal Rafael Merry del Val, Vatican State, Thursday, August 11, 1904.

as far as his house and, that same night, to give the pope a detailed account of the trip and of the reception reserved for the cardinal.[45] During these stays, Pius X continued to send signed notes to his secretary of state. To give just one example, on August 20, 1905, he wrote, "Thank you for continually thinking of me and of the Vatican; but be certain that I want nothing more than your good health, and that Your Eminence's well-being has an admirable influence on my morale and comfort."[46]

The solicitude of Pius X regarding his secretary of state did not stop there. Every year on the feast of St. Rafael, the pope sent a few affectionate and grateful words to him, accompanied by a present.[47] The first year, he wrote:

To Our dear son Cardinal Merry del Val, whose excellent services rendered to Us and to the Church We have well tried, praying with all our strength to the Lord that he will celebrate for many years with happiness and joy the feast of St. Rafael Archangel, for whom he has been named and who is his patron; in token of Our appreciation and Our personal goodwill, with great affection We send to him the Apostolic Benediction.[48]

The following year he wrote:

45. Cenci, *Il cardinale Raffaele Merry del Val*, 215–17.

46. Cited in Cenci, *Il cardinale Raffaele Merry del Val*, 216, letter from Pius X to Cardinal Rafael Merry del Val, August 20, 1905.

47. Cenci, *Il cardinale Raffaele Merry del Val*, 229.

48. Cited in Cenci, *Il cardinale Raffaele Merry del Val*, 229–30, letter from Pius X to Cardinal Rafael Merry del Val, October 24, 1904.

To Our dear son Cardinal Merry del Val who wisely and conscientiously fulfills the duties of secretary of Our public affairs, on this day when he celebrated the annual feast of his heavenly patron, in token of Our appreciation and of Our personal goodwill, We send this wish with Our Apostolic Benediction: "That a good angel of God accompany you and happily arrange all the happens to you ... so that you will always be in joy." (Tob. V)[49]

Each year, the ritual was renewed. A final example, a note that the pope wrote to him in 1909 and in which his sentiments regarding his secretary of state are particularly explicit, says,

May the Archangel Rafael, valiant doctor and faithful guide, obtain for you from Our Lord, for many years, all the graces that you would desire. That is my wish for you with gratitude and goodwill that cannot be expressed with words.[50]

In the same manner, for the twenty-fifth anniversary of the first Mass of the cardinal, Pius X gave to him a valuable pectoral cross and chain, along with the following words:

49. ASCAES, Stati Ecclesiastici, 1903–1904, Posizione 1267, Fascicolo 429 (Rome 1903–12), letter from Puis X to Cardinal Rafael Merry del Val, Tuesday October 24, 1905. Pius X adapted the quotation from the book of Tobias (Tb 5:27): "For I believe that the good angel of God doth accompany him, and doth order all things well that are done about him, so that he shall return to us with joy." The original Latin text is: "Credo enim quod angelus Dei bonus comitetur ei, et bene disponat omnia quæ circa eum geruntur, ita ut cum gaudio revertatur ad nos."

50. Cited in Cenci, *Il cardinale Raffaele Merry del Val*, 231, letter from Pius X to Cardinal Rafael Merry del Val, October 24, 1909.

If, due to Your Reverend Eminence's modesty, it is not possible to know the precise day of the 25th anniversary of your first Mass, I hope that you will appreciate, all the same, the best wishes I wholeheartedly offer for your golden anniversary, not only priestly, but episcopal and cardinal, and that you will accept this small sign of my gratitude for the scholarly, affectionate, and selfless help and sacrifices that you have given in the government of the Church.[51]

The thoughtfulness of Pius X toward his secretary of state was not reserved for special occasions; it was exhibited daily. For instance, if the pope needed to consult him after an audience, so as not to interrupt his work he would not call him back, but instead would send him a signed note—for instance, "To the Eminent Lord Cardinal Secretary of State with the request to study the case and respond";[52] or again, "I await however the judgment of Your Eminence: a judgment which he will give me in his own time and which I will treasure."[53] This type of correspondence went on throughout the pontificate of Pius X.

The last meeting between Pius X and his secretary of state well illustrates their sentiments for each other and the depths of the ties that united them. On August 15, 1914, after the Feast of the Assumption, Pius X "felt a

51. Cited in Cenci, *Il cardinale Raffaele Merry del Val*, 231–32, letter from Pius X to Cardinal Rafael Merry del Val, January 1, 1913.

52. Cited in Cenci, *Il cardinale Raffaele Merry del Val*, 241, letter from Pius X to Cardinal Rafael Merry del Val, s.l., s.d.

53. Cited in Cenci, *Il cardinale Raffaele Merry del Val*, 242, letter from Pius X to Cardinal Rafael Merry del Val, Thursday, March 9, 1905.

little unwell."[54] His malaise did not upset anyone; it was attributed to the oppressive heat. On August 18, Cardinal Merry del Val was to visit the pope for an audience, but, being indisposed, he was not able to go himself. So he sent Msgr. Canali—who was then the substitute secretary of state—to report to the Holy Father on several urgent affairs. Upon his return, Msgr. Canali told the cardinal that Pius X "showed no symptoms of illness," and that he had said, "Monsignor, tell the Cardinal that he is well, because when he is sick, I am sick too."[55] The next morning, the pope did not arise at his usual time. Msgr. Bressan, his private secretary, went to see him. He "found him to be feverish and unwell."[56] At around 10:00 a.m., the sovereign pontiff was in grave crisis. Upon hearing this, Cardinal Merry del Val hurried over to the bedside of the Holy Father, whom he found to be "breathing with great difficulty."[57] Pius X squeezed his hand strongly, saying only, "Eminence, Eminence!"[58] The cardinal then passed the rest of the day in the neighboring chamber, with other close collaborators of the pope.[59] Around 11:30 p.m., he once more entered the chamber of the dying man. This was the last time the two men saw each other. This final meeting was described by Cardinal Merry del Val in his book *Impressions et Souvenirs*:

54. Merry del Val, *Pie X*, 111.
55. Merry del Val, *Pie X*, 111.
56. Merry del Val, *Pie X*, 111.
57. Merry del Val, *Pie X*, 112.
58. Merry del Val, *Pie X*, 113.
59. Merry del Val, *Pie X*, 115.

Around 11:30 p.m., I entered into his chamber. Suddenly, he turned towards me, following me with his penetrating look while I went to the foot of his bed. He raised his arms as if to greet me and when I sat down near him, he took me by the hand and squeezed it with such force that I was amazed. The Pope stared at me intensely, his eyes gazing into mine. How I would have loved to be able to read his thoughts at that moment and to hear his voice while we were speaking to each other with our eyes! Was the Holy Father thinking of the long years that I had passed with him, of our confident relationship, of what we had suffered together? Did he look through a last salute to console me in my grief that I was making myself hide? God alone knows.

In that way, he kept my hand in his for forty minutes. From time to time, he loosened his clasp to give me a little caress then he retook my hand.

At the end, fatigued, he put his head on the cushions and closed his eyes.

It seemed to me that Pius X had said his goodbyes to me! I will never forget the final scene of our separation! It is present in my mind as it unfolded that memorable night. It seemed to me to bring to life the words of St. Lawrence that we read several days ago in the breviary:

Quo progrederis sine filio, Pater? Quo, Sacerdos sancte, sine Ministro properas? Where are you going, Father, without your son? Where are you moving to, priest, without your servant?[60]

Around midnight, Cardinal Merry del Val left to take his rest. He was convinced that the pope "would survive sev-

---

60. Merry del Val, *Pie X*, 116–17.

eral more hours." One hour later, they called him. He had not yet arrived in Pius X's chamber when the pope passed away.[61] The cardinal's sorrow was immense. The archives retain several letters sent by him after the death of the pontiff that reveal all his suffering. For example, several days later he wrote to his great friend Msgr. Joseph Broadhead, "The blow has been a terrible one for me and my heart is fairly broken. You see, I loved him with every fiber of my soul; he was more than a father to me and I feel as if I could not live without him. He was indeed a saint."[62] Several days later, to a devout person to whom he gave spiritual direction, he wrote:

I have suffered very much and I still suffer very much; this sorrow will remain in my heart until the end of my life. God will keep watch over the Church, but the personal loss of one who was for me more than a father and friend, of a holy pontiff to whom I had given all my strength and who had opened to me the immense treasure of his great heart, this loss for me is irreparable, it will never be compensated. So, help me with the charity of your prayers.[63]

Sources show that the relationship between the two men was founded on a mutual admiration. Pius X considered Rafael Merry del Val to be a man specifically formed and

61. Merry del Val, *Pie X*, 118.

62. Ushaw College Library, Merry del Val papers, UC/P17/31, letter from Cardinal Rafael Merry del Val to Msgr. Joseph Broadhead, s.l., Sunday September 27, 1914.

63. Cited in Cenci, *Il cardinale Raffaele Merry del Val*, 246, letter from Cardinal Rafael Merry del Val to a devout person to whom he gave spiritual direction, Wednesday, September 30, 1914.

prepared for this job, but who also worked hard and without compromise. For these reasons Pius X appointed him secretary of state and wanted to keep him near him. Further, Pius X judged, as he said explicitly to a cardinal, that Rafael Merry del Val was a "saint."[64] For his part, Rafael did not think any less of the pope, whom he admired for his supernatural virtues as well as his human qualities. Underlying it all, there was immense respect and great esteem between the two men, sentiments that turned into a deep, supernatural friendship that seemed to flow from the fact that their hearts beat in unison for the Church.

In retrospect, the relationship between Pius X and his secretary of state was characterized as having a great mutual trust. Cardinal Merry del Val mentioned this "trusting relationship" in the account of his last meeting with the pope.[65] While Rafael Merry del Val had an unlimited devotion to Pius X, displaying it through the faithful execution of his directives and by conforming himself to his will, the pope showed a great sensitivity and paternal attention toward his secretary of state. Camille Bellaigue, private chamberlain of the Cape and Sword of Pius X, who knew both men well, wrote in his personal memoirs of the pope:

During the papacy of Pope St. Pius X, I had some occasions to work with Cardinal Merry del Val. . . . Every opportunity I had, I served this great servant of the greatest of masters the best I could. And like his master, loved him. I can still hear Pius X

64. Cenci, *Il cardinale Raffaele Merry del Val*, 138.
65. Merry del Val, *Pie X*, 116–17.

saying to me, "Separating us from Cardinal Merry del Val! I would rather separate myself from my head! How can we do without him?"[66]

The relationship between the two men was so close that history and historians have not been able to disassociate the names of Pope St. Pius X and Cardinal Merry del Val.

66. Cited in Cenci, *Il cardinale Raffaele Merry del Val*, 152.

3

SECRETARY OF THE HOLY OFFICE (1914–1930)

.

A FTER THE DEATH of Pius X on August 20, 1914,[1] and the election of Benedict XV on September 3,[2] a new period opened in the life of Cardinal Merry del Val. He was replaced as secretary of state by Cardinal Domenico Ferrata[3] and named secretary of the Supreme Sacred Congregation of the Holy Office on October 14, 1914.[4] In this chapter, we consider his place and responsibilities in this congregation, the duties that were ultimately conferred on him, the last honors he received, and finally, his mysterious death.

1. *Acta Apostolicae Sedis* (*AAS*), year 6, vol. 6, no. 12 (August 20, 1914): 405.
2. *AAS*, year 6, vol. 6, no. 14 (September 3, 1914): 457.
3. *AAS*, year 6, vol. 6, no. 15 (September 17, 1914): 511.
4. *AAS*, year 6, vol. 6, no. 16 (October 16, 1914): 525.

Rafael Merry del Val and the Congregation of the Holy Office

The Sacred Congregation of the Holy Office was the successor of the Sacred Congregation of the Roman and Universal Inquisition founded by Paul III in 1542.[5] It was reformed by Pius X in 1908 and given the name of Sacred Congregation of the Holy Office.[6] Later, in 1965, it was reformed again and became the Congregation for the Doctrine of the Faith.[7]

The Sacred Congregation of the Holy Office (1908–65) had only seven successive secretaries. Rafael Merry del Val was the third, after Cardinal Rampolla, who died on December 16, 1913,[8] and Cardinal Ferrata, who died on October 10, 1914,[9] having been named secretary of state

5. Paul III, Constitution *Licet ab initio,* 21 juillet 1542, *Bullarum privilegiorum ac diplomatum Romanorum Pontificum amplissima collectio Cui accessere Pontificum omnium Vitae, Notae, et Indices opportuni: Opera et Studio Caroli Cocquelines, Tomus quartus Pars prima, Ab Hadriano VI ad Paulum IV scilicet ab Anno 1521 ad 1559* (Rome: Typis, et Sumptibus Hieronymi Mainardi, Superiorum Facultate, 1745), 211–12.

6. *Acta Sanctae Sedis (ASS)*, vol. 41 (1908): 425–27.

7. *AAS*, year 57, vol. 57, no. 14 (December 30, 1965): 952–55. On the subject of this congregation, see, among others, Adriano Prosperi, *Tribunali della coscienza: Inquisitori, confessori, missionari* (Turin: Einaudi 1996); John Tedeschi, *Il giudice e l'eretico: Studi sull'Inquisizione romana* (Milan: Vita e Pensiero, 1997); Agostino Borromeo, ed., *L'inquisizione: Atti del Simposio internazionale (Città del Vaticano, 29–31 ottobre 1998)* (Città del Vaticano: Biblioteca Apostolica Vaticana, 2003); Andrea del Col, *L'inquisizione in Italia dal XII al XXI secolo* (Milan: Mondadori, 2006); Adriano Prosperi, ed., *Dizionario storico dell'Inquisizione*, 4 vols. (Pisa: Edizioni della Normale, 2010).

8. *AAS*, year 5, vol. 5, no. 18 (December 20, 1913): 544.

9. *AAS*, year 6, vol. 6, no. 16 (October 16, 1914): 532.

a little more than a month before, on September 4.[10] This left the position of secretary of the Congregation of the Holy Office open, and Benedict XV entrusted it to Cardinal Merry del Val.

If we take into consideration only the secretaries of the Congregation of the Holy Office, from 1908 to 1965, the median age at the time of each one's nomination was sixty-six years. Rafael Merry del Val was appointed at forty-nine years of age. He was the youngest one to be named, and, as with the secretaries of state, he was the first non-Italian to accede to this position.[11] However, his designation as head of the Holy Office was less surprising than his nomination as secretary of state in 1903. First, his predecessor as secretary of state, Cardinal Rampolla, had moved into the same position after his term as secretary of state. Moreover, it would have been difficult to give him a second-level post after his eleven years at the summit of the government of the church.

To understand the responsibilities of Cardinal Merry del Val as the head of the Congregation of the Holy Office, it is necessary to examine Pius X's reforms of the duties of the office. According to the constitution *Sapienti consilio* of June 29, 1908, the duties of the Holy Office were to "safeguard doctrine concerning faith and morals" and "to judge heresy and other crimes which contain a suspicion of heresy." The Holy Office was also in charge of

10. *AAS*, year 6, vol 6, no. 15 (September 17, 1914), 511.
11. Calculations based on data from the website http://www.catholic-hierarchy.org [consulted April 8, 2015].

the question of indulgences, and it had a right to review doctrinal questions related to the sacraments.[12] In 1917, Benedict XV abolished the Congregation of the Index and transferred its jurisdiction to the Holy Office, from which he then removed the charge for indulgences, so as to avoid this merger excessively increasing the quantity of its work.[13] Thus, the condemnation of writings considered to be dangerous to Catholics became the responsibility of the congregation directed by Cardinal Merry del Val.

Final Duties and Honors

After his appointment as the head of the Holy Office, which in order of precedence was the most important of the Roman congregations,[14] Cardinal Merry del Val received other posts from Benedict XV. In December 1915, the sovereign pontiff named him a member of both the Sacred Ceremonial Congregation and the Sacred Congregation for the Propagation of the Faith, as well as president of the Pontifical Academy of the Catholic Religion.[15] The following year, he became a member of the Sacred

12. Pius X, "Constitutio Apostolica de Romana Curia," *AAS*, year 1, vol. 1 (1909): 9.

13. Benedict XV, "Motu proprio Alloquentes proxime," *AAS*, year 9, vol. 9 (1917): 167.

14. Pius X, "Constitutio Apostolica de Romana Curia," 9.

15. *Annuario Pontificio per l'anno 1916* (Rome: Tipografia Poliglotta Vaticana, 1916), 41, 332, 346, 602.

Congregation for the Propagation of the Faith for Affairs of Eastern Rite.[16]

Rafael Merry del Val received honors as well as assignments from Benedict XV. The most important was certainly his appointment as pontifical legate to Assisi for the first centenary of the discovery of the body of St. Francis and for the catechetical congress of Umbria in 1920.[17] Six years later, in 1926, this honor was renewed by Pius XI, who named him pontifical legate to Assisi for the 700th anniversary of the death of St. Francis.[18] Under Benedict XV and Pius XI, contrary to the claims of some, Cardinal Merry del Val was not banished to the depths of the Curia. Certainly, his term as the head of the Secretariat of State was not renewed, but that was not surprising. History shows that a new pope often names a new secretary of state, and Merry del Val's politics were so aligned to those of Pius X that Benedict XV, who was more of the "Rampollian" orientation,[19] would have had difficulty keeping him as secretary of state. Indeed, Car-

16. *Annuario Pontificio per l'anno 1917* (Rome: Tipografia Poliglotta Vaticana, 1917), 348.

17. Cenci, *Il cardinale Raffaele Merry del Val*, 524–27.

18. *Osservatore Romano*, no. 231, lunedì-martedì, 4–5 ottobre 1926; *Osservatore Romano*, no. 232, mercoledì 6 ottobre 1926.

19. *Vaticana beatificationis et canonizationis Servi Dei Raphaëlis Card. Merry del Val ... : Summarium super dubio...* (1957), 141, testimony of Canon Francesco Rossi Stockalper; Archivio Centrale dello Stato (ACS), Ministero dell'Interno, Direzione Generale della Pubblica Sicurezza, Divisione Polizia Politica, b 828, "Mery [sic] Del Val Raffaele," "Profilo del Cardinale Raffaele Mery [sic] del Val," Rome, August 7, 1929; see also Yves Chiron, *Benoît XV: Le pape de la paix* (Paris: Perrin, 2014), 34–35, 37, 45, 49, 51, 62–63, 65, 69, 79–80, 114–15, 125, 129.

dinal Merry del Val was not completely removed from political affairs, as he remained a member of the Congregation for Extraordinary Ecclesiastical Affairs.[20] Hence
he always had his say in the diplomatic affairs of the
Holy See.

Relationship with Benedict XV and Pius XI

Cardinal Merry del Val's relationships with Benedict XV
and Pius XI were not the same as that with Pius X. For
all that, could one say that they were bad, strained, or
sometimes difficult, as some have claimed?[21] Let us examine this more closely: If these relationships had been
so objectionable, the later popes could have given Cardinal Merry del Val purely honorific posts. They never did

20. *Annuario Pontificio per l'anno 1915* (Rome: Tipografia Poliglotta Vaticana, 1915), 345.

21. See, for example, *Les carnets du cardinal Alfred Baudrillart (1er janvier 1919–31 décembre 1921)*, text introduced, set up, and annotated by Paul
Christophe (Paris: Éditions du Cerf, 2000), 865; *Les carnets du cardinal Alfred
Baudrillart (1er janvier 1922–12 avril 1925)* (Paris: Éditions du Cerf, 2001), 414,
642, 652, 702; *Les carnets du cardinal Alfred Baudrillart (26 décembre 1928–12
février 1932)* (Paris: Éditions du Cerf, 2003), 584; *Vaticana beatificationis et
canonizationis Servi Dei Raphaëlis Card. Merry del Val: Summarium super dubio
An signanda sit Commissio introductionis Causæ in casu et ad effectum de quo
agitur*, 1957; ACS, Ministero dell'Interno, Direzione Generale della Pubblica Sicurezza, Divisione Polizia Politica, b 828, "Mery [sic] Del Val Raffaele,"
"Profilo del Cardinale Raffaele Mery [sic] del Val," Rome, August 7, 1929; note
"Dal nostro corrispondente Vaticano," Rome, September 7, 1929; note, Città
del Vaticano, October 19, 1919.

that. Nevertheless, the rumors flying around concerning the tumultuous relations between the former secretary of state of Pius X and the two popes who followed him originate from sufficiently numerous and credible sources that one should not dismiss such assertions out of hand. Let us therefore examine the relationship of Cardinal Merry del Val with each of these two popes a little more closely.

Before the election of Benedict XV, Giacomo della Chiesa and Rafael Merry del Val had worked together for a long time. When the latter was named secretary of state, Msgr. della Chiesa became the deputy secretary of state.[22] He was confirmed in this position,[23] which he kept until his appointment as archbishop of Bologna in 1907.[24] For about five years, he was one of Cardinal Merry del Val's closest collaborators. When mentioning his relationship with the cardinal during this period, Benedict XV told his friend Baron Monti that it had been "correct, but certainly not close."[25] In his testimony for the beatification process for Cardinal Merry del Val, Cardinal Canali, who assisted him and lived with him for around thirty years,[26] said that the work and personal relationship between Cardinal Merry del Val and Msgr. della Chiesa "was always marked by the most manifest sincerity and cordiality." He

22. *La Gerarchia Cattolica 1903* (Rome: Tipografia Vaticana, 1903), 793.
23. *La Gerarchia Cattolica 1904* (Rome: Tipografia Vaticana, 1904), 489.
24. *La Gerarchia Cattolica 1908* (Rome: Tipografia Vaticana, 1908), 125.
25. Cited in Chiron, *Benoît XV*, 80.
26. *Vaticana beatificationis et canonizationis Servi Dei Raphaëlis Card. Merry del Val* (1957), testimony of Cardinal Nicola Canali, 264–65.

added, "In the years of work common to the Secretariat of State, i.e., from August 1903 to October 1907, I can say that there were never any differences or disagreements, but the greatest mutual understanding."[27] Cardinal Canali also affirmed that "raised to the pontifical throne, Benedict XV always showed towards the Servant of God delightfully tender sentiments and respect, desiring from the beginning to publicly demonstrate his sentiments to him with several official acts."[28]

Other testimonies gathered for the inquiry would have one think that the reality was perhaps slightly different. So, for example, Alberto Serafini, canon of St. Peter's Basilica, stated that in the relationship between Cardinal Merry del Val and Giacomo della Chiesa, from the time when he was deputy secretary of state, there was always "a reserve that only the diplomatic professionalism of the two could prevent from becoming openly hostile," which he deduced from a hint made to him by the future Benedict XV when he was archbishop of Bologna.[29] Francesco Rossi Stockalper, canon of the basilica of St. Mary Major, said of Merry del Val:

Msgr. della Chiesa saw Cardinal Rampolla as a should-have-been-pope. Because of that, he did not look with approval on the Servant of God in the position of secretary of state. Msgr.

27. *Vaticana beatificationis et canonizationis*, testimony of Cardinal Nicola Canali, 343.
28. *Vaticana beatificationis et canonizationis*, testimony of Cardinal Nicola Canali, 346.
29. *Vaticana beatificationis et canonizationis*, testimony of Canon Alberto Serafini, 152.

della Chiesa often used this expression, "But Cardinal Rampolla would never have done that!" However, the Servant of God, being well aware of that, never complained and continued to treat Msgr. della Chiesa kindly.[30]

It is likely that this appraisal corresponds to reality. Indeed, all the consulted testimonies underline the respect Cardinal Merry del Val had for Benedict XV. For example, Cardinal Giuseppe Pizzardo stated:

In the relationship between the Servant of God and Msgr. della Chiesa, there was nothing abnormal. . . . I never heard, either directly or indirectly, a word from the Servant of God either against or in favor of della Chiesa. When della Chiesa was elected pope taking the name of Benedict XV, I heard the Servant of God speak of the new pope with great respect and veneration and on that there is no doubt.[31]

In addition, different letters sent to Cardinal Merry del Val by Benedict XV, which can be found in the archives, indubitably show a courteous and deferential relationship.[32]

30. *Vaticana beatificationis et canonizationis*, testimony of Canon Francesco Rossi Stockalper, 141.

31. *Vaticana beatificationis et canonizationis*, testimony of Cardinal Giuseppe Pizzardo, 222.

32. For example, Archivio Segreto Vaticano (ASV), Segreteria di Stato, Spogli di Cardinali e Officiali di Curia, Rafael Merry del Val, busta 5, fol. 405, letter from Benedict XV to Cardinal Rafael Merry del Val, Vatican, November 12, 1914; fol. 406, letter from Benedict XV to Cardinal Rafael Merry del Val, s.l., December 2, 1914; fol. 408, letter from Benedict XV to Cardinal Rafael Merry del Val, s.l., April 14, 1915; fol. 409, letter from Benedict XV to Cardinal Rafael Merry del Val, Vatican, March 7, 1916; fol. 418, letter from Benedict XV to Cardinal Rafael Merry del Val, s.l., April 24, 1918; fol. 421, letter from Benedict XV to Cardinal Rafael Merry del Val, Vatican, September 5,

And then, there is a very specific event that demonstrates Cardinal Merry del Val's attitude toward Benedict XV and the way in which the latter considered him. This concerns the French cultural associations, which had been disallowed and condemned by Pius X in 1906. In 1921, France and the Holy See had opened negotiations on the subject of these associations in view of reaching an accord. Cardinal Merry del Val, like several French bishops, was opposed to these associations. Benedict XV asked Canon Ferdinand Renaud—who played an important role in this affair—to try to convince the recalcitrant people of the legitimacy of the diocesan cultural associations. Ferdinand Renaud then proposed to Benedict XV to go see Cardinal Merry del Val. According to the testimony of the canon, the pope answered him, "It is useless ... the Cardinal is not in favor of the diocesan [associations], you see, but it is not with him that we will have difficulties: HE IS A SAINT, he will never embarrass us."[33] This anecdote corresponds exactly to Cardinal Merry del Val's spirit of submission toward the popes whom he served.

Tension and misunderstandings were also reported to have occurred in his relationship with Pius XI.[34] There

1918; fol. 423, letter from Benedict XV to Cardinal Rafael Merry del Val, s.l., June 26, 1920.

33. Pontificio Colegio Español de San José, Archivo Merry del Val (PCESJ, AMDV), fol. 6014, statement of Ferdinand Renaud, Paris, November 5, 1956.

34. For example, *Vaticana beatificationis et canonizationis Servi Dei Raphaëlis Card. Merry del Val* (1957), 132, testimony of Cesidio Lolli, editor of *L'Osservatore Romano*; ACS, Ministero dell'Interno, Direzione Generale della Pubblica Sicurezza, Divisione Polizia Politica, b 828, "Mery [sic] Del Val Raf-

certainly was disagreement between Pius XI and Cardinal Merry del Val. The most notable that comes to mind is the question of the condemnation of *Action Française*.[35] For example, in a note concerning an audience he had with Pius XI on that subject, the cardinal wrote, "The Pope treated me like a young schoolboy."[36] In a draft letter on the subject, he wrote, "I wholeheartedly submit to his superior judgment and will conform myself scrupulously to it as it is my strict duty."[37]

As regards the relationship between the cardinal and Pius XI, it is interesting to note the following anecdote.

faele," note "Dal nostro corrispondente Vaticano," Rome, September 7, 1929; note, Città del Vaticano, October 19, 1919.

35. ASV, Segreteria di Stato, Spogli di Cardinali e Officiali di Curia, Rafael Merry del Val, busta 6, fol. 731, note from Cardinal Rafael Merry del Val regarding an audience he had with Pius XI on the question of *Action Française*, February 23, 1927; ACS, Ministero dell'Interno, Direzione Generale della Pubblica Sicurezza, Divisione Polizia Politica, b 828, "Mery [sic] Del Val Raffaele," Rome, note of 3 March 3, 1930; *Vaticana beatificationis et canonizationis Servi Dei Raphaëlis Card. Merry del Val* (1957), 137, testimony of Cardinal Ernesto Ruffini: "Un giorno vidi il Servo di Dio particolarmente afflitto dopo un'udienza del Santo Padre Pio XI, però non si lamentava, non reagiva, piuttosto mostrava un profondo dispiacere, credo in seguito a qualche parola forte dettagli dal Papa Pio XI: allora era viva la famosa questione dell'*Action Française*"; *Les carnets du cardinal Alfred Baudrillart (13 avril 1925–25 décembre 1928)*, text introduced, set up, and annotated by Paul Christophe (Paris: Éditions du Cerf, 2002), 619, 627, 908.

36. ASV, Segreteria di Stato, Spogli di Cardinali e Officiali di Curia, Rafael Merry del Val, busta 6, fol. 731, note of Cardinal Rafael Merry del Val regarding an audience that he had with Pius XI on the question of *Action Française*, February 23, 1927.

37. ASV, Segreteria di Stato, Spogli di Cardinali e Officiali di Curia, Rafael Merry del Val, busta 6, fol. 732, draft of a letter from Cardinal Rafael Merry del Val to Pius XI, s.l., February 24, 1927.

On February 23, 1927, Cardinal Merry del Val wrote to Camille Bellaigue, private chamberlain to the Cape and Sword of Pius X, Benedict XV, and Pius XI,[38] to inform him of the following event:

His Holiness had [received] a typewritten page, signed I think, in which it literally said that I had written a letter to you in which I had said to you that Pope Pius XI "is as stubborn as a mule." You know me well enough to know that never would such an expression come out of my mouth nor even less from my pen. This is not my style. This event has created grave consequences for me and I am suffering greatly because of it. Would you please do me the service of writing both to His Holiness and to the Cardinal Secretary of State and issue a formal refutation, because I am the victim of an odious lie.[39]

After having read this letter closely, Camille Bellaigue wrote the following telegram to Cardinal Merry del Val: "Filled with sorrow and outrage, I am writing immediately. More loyal than ever."[40] Then in a letter to Pius XI, dated February 27, 1927, he refuted the allegations using the following words:

38. ASV, Segreteria di Stato, Spogli di Cardinali e Officiali di Curia, Rafael Merry del Val, busta 6, fol. 733, 2, copy of a letter from Camille Bellaigue to Pius XI, Paris, February 27, 1927.

39. ASV, Segreteria di Stato, Spogli di Cardinali e Officiali di Curia, Rafael Merry del Val, busta 6, fol. 733, letter from Cardinal Merry del Val to Camille Bellaigue, Rome, February 23, 1927.

40. ASV, Segreteria di Stato, Spogli di Cardinali e Officiali di Curia, Rafael Merry del Val, busta 6, fol. 734, telegram from Camille Bellaigue to Cardinal Rafael Merry del Val, Paris, February 26, 1927.

Your Holiness had received an anonymous, or perhaps signed, typewritten page, in which it is claimed that His Eminence Cardinal Merry del Val had literally written to me, in terms that I scarcely dare to report: that Pope Pius XI "is as stubborn as a mule." Against this vile slander, injurious not only to the elevated, admirable personality of Cardinal Merry del Val, but beneath, very beneath it, I, myself, protest to Your Holiness, with all the strength of my indignation and my sorrow.[41]

Several days later, on March 6, Cardinal Gasparri wrote to Cardinal Merry del Val to inform him that this letter had satisfied Pius XI and that the pope considered the incident to be closed.[42] The next day, March 7, Cardinal Merry del Val wrote the following words to Camille Bellaigue:

I knew that you would not hesitate to help me, but I am still grateful to you for it. Your letter, so fine and so honorable, has been delivered and appears to have produced its effect. It hurts me to see that my own refutation was not enough. How relentlessly they seek to ruin me, using every means, even the most despicable. May God forgive them, as I forgive, and may He deign to draw good from evil. Thank you again with all my heart.[43]

41. ASV, Segreteria di Stato, Spogli di Cardinali e Officiali di Curia, Rafael Merry del Val, busta 6, fol. 733, 2, copy of a letter from Camille Bellaigue to Pius XI, Paris, February 27, 1927.

42. ASV, Segreteria di Stato, Spogli di Cardinali e Officiali di Curia, Rafael Merry del Val, busta 6, fol. 735, letter from Cardinal Pietro Gasparri to Cardinal Rafael Merry del Val, Segreteria di Stato, March 6, 1927.

43. ASV, Segreteria di Stato, Spogli di Cardinali e Officiali di Curia, Rafael Merry del Val, busta 6, fol. 736, letter from Cardinal Rafael Merry del Val to Camille Bellaigue, s.l., March 7, 1927.

Otherwise, Pius XI well appreciated Cardinal Merry del Val. According to his testimony, the pope said to Msgr. Nicola Canali, "You, Monsignor, have had from God the truly special and extraordinary grace of living in contact with an ecclesiastical personage of so much valor and so much piety."[44] The day after the death of the cardinal, Thursday, February 27, 1930, Msgr. Canali as usual went to see Pius XI for an audience concerning the affairs of the Holy Office. According to his testimony, he was received in the following manner by the pope:

Having barely arrived at the Holy Father's workplace, contrary to the usual custom, he rose and warmly embraced me, exclaiming with emotion, "What a great sadness We have for the Church, for the Holy See and for you in particular!" expressing to me great condolences and declaring that he had prayed and will continue to pray for him [Cardinal Merry del Val], and he recited the *De profundis* with me.[45]

A note from the secret police at the time revealed the following information on the reaction of Pius XI when he learned of the death of the cardinal:

The pope was left stunned by the death of Merry del Val. He said to Cardinal Pacelli and to Msgr. Canali, who had hastened to inform him of the fatal news, "But how is this possible? Here is a letter from him that arrived several hours ago in which he thanked me for the very nice lamb that we

44. *Vaticana beatificationis et canonizationis Servi Dei Raphaëlis Card. Merry del Val*, testimony of Cardinal Nicola Canali, 348.

45. *Vaticana beatificationis et canonizationis Servi Dei Raphaëlis Card. Merry del Val*, testimony of Cardinal Nicola Canali, 349.

had sent to him Sunday in honor of the baptism of our great-niece."—And, overcome with tears, he could not convince himself of the sudden loss of the illustrious Cardinal! He dismissed everyone, recollected himself in prayer for the soul of the deceased, did not want to eat, and passed all night from Wednesday to Thursday without resting, meditating and sighing, his chamberlain told us, as if he felt the tragic departure for the afterlife was also imminent for him.[46]

Then he added that Pius XI agreed to the cardinal's wish expressed in his will[47] of being buried near the body of his beloved friend Pius X.[48] Here is how that was reported in a note to the Italian political police:

Sunday morning, Msgr. Caccia went before the pope showing him this very great testamentary desire of the deceased Cardinal and to solicit from him the necessary approval. He added that if it were not possible to fulfill it, the Cardinal prayed that his sepulcher be put in St. Praxedes, his cardinalate titular church. The pope answered that he would think about it and make his answer that evening. But, a few minutes after Msgr. Caccia had left, Pius XI called a manservant and ordered him summon Msgr. Caccia immediately. Once the monsignor was before him, the pontiff said to him, "You know, Monsignor, we thought about it. We were undecided because we also wanted to reserve for us upon dying the same

46. ACS, Ministero dell'Interno, Direzione Generale della Pubblica Sicurezza, Divisione Polizia Politica, b 828, "Mery [sic] Del Val Raffaele," Città del Vaticano, note of February 28, 1930.

47. PCESJ, AMDV, fol. 895–98, testament of Cardinal Rafael Merry del Val, Città del Vaticano, Rome, July 15, 1928.

48. PCESJ, AMDV, fol. 897.

fate as that claimed by the deceased Cardinal, that is, for our grave to be near to Pius X. We believed that there would be no place for us as well, but in rethinking the situation, we are sure that there will be a place. So tell Msgr. Canali and the noble brothers of Merry del Val that there is no difficulty on our part."

These details have been reported to us directly by Msgr. Caccia.[49]

In another note to the political police, it is mentioned that, according to Cardinal Laurenti, nobody would have thought that Pius XI would have been so genuinely afflicted by the death of the cardinal and that he had given the highest and most sincere praise regarding him.[50] This information was confirmed by Msgr. Canali, who reacted to the following words of Pius XI: "The Church has suffered a great loss with the death of Cardinal Merry del Val, and his merits are more appreciated after his death."[51] These words did not please Msgr. Canali, who declared,

Vain words ... after so many years of having the ability and worth of such a man remain so neglected and unknown. There is no explanation for a pope who boasts of venerating

49. ACS, Ministero dell'Interno, Direzione Generale della Pubblica Sicurezza, Divisione Polizia Politica, b 828, "Mery [sic] Del Val Raffaele," Città del Vaticano, note of March 4, 1930.

50. ACS, Ministero dell'Interno, Direzione Generale della Pubblica Sicurezza, Divisione Polizia Politica, b 828, "Mery [sic] Del Val Raffaele," Città del Vaticano, note of March 8, 1930.

51. ACS, Ministero dell'Interno, Direzione Generale della Pubblica Sicurezza, Divisione Polizia Politica, b 828, "Mery [sic] Del Val Raffaele," Città del Vaticano, note of March 22, 1930.

the memory of Pius X and of very much appreciating his religious papacy, who could sideline this Cardinal who faithfully represented Pius X.[52]

These remarks are contradictory to the testimony that he made for the process of beatification for Cardinal Merry del Val, in which he said, "Concerning the relationship between the Servant of God and Pope Pius XI, I can attest in the most explicit and direct manner that they were always marked with sentiments of profound understanding and reciprocal cordiality."[53] That did not exactly correspond to the reality, as the archives show. On the other hand, the cardinal submitted to the pope as a matter of principle, as shown notably in the bequest in his last will and testament, "I leave to the reigning pope my pectoral cross with amethysts and a cameo of the Blessed Virgin, with its chain, given to me by Leo XIII, as a sign of my unconditional attachment to the vicar of Jesus Christ and to the chair of St. Peter."[54]

Furthermore, can it be said that Cardinal Merry del Val had been sidelined after the death of Pius X? It seems not. Under Benedict XV and under Pius XI, as under Pius X, Rafael Merry del Val was one of the most powerful men in the church. When he died, during an appendec-

52. ACS, Ministero dell'Interno, Direzione Generale della Pubblica Sicurezza, Divisione Polizia Politica, b 828, "Mery [sic] Del Val Raffaele," Città del Vaticano, note of March 22, 1930.

53. *Vaticana beatificationis et canonizationis Servi Dei Raphaëlis Card. Merry del Val,* 347–48, testimony of Cardinal Nicola Canali.

54. PCESJ, AMDV, fol. 897, testament of Cardinal Rafael Merry del Val, Città del Vaticano, Rome, July 15, 1928.

tomy on February 26, 1930,[55] he was a man at the height of his glory, with great responsibility, and showered with honors. He was a cardinal, archpriest of St. Peter's Basilica, secretary of the Congregation of the Holy Office, prefect of the Congregation of the Fabric of St. Peters, and a member of the following congregations: the Congregation of the Consistory, the Congregation for the Eastern Churches, the Congregation of the Council, the Congregation for the Propagation of the Faith, the Congregation of Rites, the Congregation of Ceremonies, the Congregation for Extraordinary Ecclesiastical Affairs, and the Congregation for Seminaries and Universities. Furthermore, he was a member of the following commissions: the Pontifical Commission for Biblical Studies, the Cardinals Commission for l'Opera Praeservationis Fidei in Roma,[56] and the Cardinals Commission for the Administration of the Goods of the Holy See. He was also president of the Pontifical Academy of the Catholic Religion.[57] In addition, it should be noted that he was the cardinal protector of twenty-nine religious institutions.[58]

55. *AAS*, year 22, vol. 22, no. 3 (March 3, 1930): 152.

56. The Roman Work for the Preservation of the Faith.

57. *Annuario Pontificio per l'anno 1930* (Città del Vaticano: Tipografia Poliglotta Vaticana, 1930), 37.

58. *Annuario Pontificio per l'anno 1930*. Rafael Merry del Val was cardinal protector of the following communities: "della Congr. Missionaria di S. Giuseppe di Mill Hill,—delle Figlie della Croce, di Liegi,—delle Serve di Gesù, di Bilbao,—dell'Istituto di Santa Maria (delle Dame Inglesi),—dell'Istituto Nazionale Teutonico di S. Maria dell'Anima,—delle Suore del Terz'Ordine Francescano in La Crosse,—dell'Arciconfraternita del Carmine in Trastevere,—dell'Ordine di Frati Minori Conventuali,—delle Dame Catechiste

The Death of Cardinal Merry del Val

The unexpected death of Cardinal Merry del Val provoked great shock. A note by the Italian political police, dated the day of his death, used the following words: "The death of Merry del Val was a bolt from the blue."[59] No one expected him to disappear so early or in such a sudden manner. He was sixty-four years old, but he was in good health; the information gathered on this subject from Msgr. Canali by the political police is clear:

No one could ever have foreseen such a tragically premature and violent death. The Cardinal had never felt such pain as an appendicitis attack, no one ever thought it would be such a catastrophic and fatal latent danger! His strong and tough disposition, his regular way of life, his love of gymnastic exercises and his constant practice, daily exercise that he

---

Spagnuole,—dei Giuseppini del Belgio, della Congr. della Carità di N. Signora d'Evron,—delle Suore della Divina Provvidenza nello Stato di Texas,—delle Suore di Carità dette 'Suore Grigie' del Canadà,—delle Suore della Carità della B. Vergine, di Dubuque,—delle Dame del Sacro Cuore,—delle Suore della Dottrina Cristiana, di Nancy,—delle Suore di Carità dell'Ospedale di S. Giacinto,—delle Suore del Terz'Ordine di S. Francesco di Oldenburg in Indiana,—delle Ancelle del Sacro Cuore e della Vergine Immac., di Siviglia,—delle Suore dell'Adorazione perpetua del SSmo Sacramento in Ronco di Ghiffa (Novara),—delle Suore della Carità di S. Carlo, di Nancy,—delle Sorelle Francescane del Terz'Ordine dell'Immac. Concezione in Joliet,—dell'Unione Internazionale delle Leghe Cattoliche Femminili,—dei Benedettini Vallombrosani,—delle Suore della Presentazione, di Madras,—del Collegio Scozzese,—dei Fratelli delle Scuole Cristiane di Lambecq (Belgio),—del Collegio Inglese in Roma,—del Collegio Beda in Roma."

59. ACS, Ministero dell'Interno, Direzione Generale della Pubblica Sicurezza, Divisione Polizia Politica, b 828, "Mery [sic] Del Val Raffaele," Rome, note of February 26, 1930.

never skipped, his balance, in a word, Msgr. Canali repeated in tears, the moral and physical balance of his existence dedicated to work, to study, to the multiple functions of his numerous responsibilities as a Cardinal, in short, everything that would lead one to believe a long and flourishing life for His Eminence. And yet, he is dead and has parted from the world in the blink of an eye![60]

The anonymous author added the note:

We too saw him and had spoken to him the Sunday before. With his usual distinction, he received us and spoke of the baptism conferred on the great niece of the Pope. Yet, he was rather tired and very busy. He invited us to come back to see him at the end of the month. Instead, we must kneel before his dead body.... We have also lost in Cardinal Mery [sic] del Val a generous and faithful protector; a polite, most amiable and trustworthy master, who never ceased showing us, explaining to us, and revealing to us, without a break, a great part of his soul in the most delicate political-religious affairs.[61]

This unforeseen death made many waves. Officially, Rafael Merry del Val died during an appendectomy. Others have claimed that he was suffocated by his dentures;[62] by

60. ACS, Ministero dell'Interno, Direzione Generale della Pubblica Sicurezza, Divisione Polizia Politica, b 828, "Mery [sic] Del Val Raffaele," Città del Vaticano, note of February 27, 1930.

61. ACS, Ministero dell'Interno, Direzione Generale della Pubblica Sicurezza, Divisione Polizia Politica, b 828, "Mery [sic] Del Val Raffaele," Città del Vaticano, note of February 27, 1930.

62. *Vaticana beatificationis et canonizationis Servi Dei Raphaëlis Card. Merry del Val* (1957), 175, testimonies of Alberto Serafini, Canon of St. Peter's Basilica; 197, and of Enrico Mascioli, adjunct director of the *Musei Lateranensi*.

his tongue, because of the drugs;[63] or through inadvertent suffocation by the surgeon.[64] On July 26, 1930, Cardinal Alfred Baudrillart, very *au courant* in the local gossip circulating around Rome, wrote in his notebook, "The Cardinal's death made a great impression; he is dead due to suffocating during the operation; some have said that they had forgotten to remove his dentures and that he had swallowed them; others, and this is more believable, that his tongue was tilted back and contracted in a way to suffocate him."[65]

The unexpected and mysterious death of Rafael Merry del Val was not questioned solely by the inner circles of the Vatican or people who had known him personally. It was also of interest to the Italian political police. In the dossier on the cardinal, which can be found in the archives of the fascist regime—and which also contained gross errors about him—there are many confidential notes on the question.[66] The first was dated February 27, 1930, the day after the cardinal's death.[67] It reported that

63. *Vaticana beatificationis et canonizationis Servi Dei Raphaëlis Card. Merry del Val* (1957), 209–10, testimony of Luigi Nardini, member of the Pious Association of the Sacred Heart of Jesus.

64. *Vaticana beatificationis et canonizationis Servi Dei Raphaëlis Card. Merry del Val* (1957), 236, testimony of Raffaele Taucci, priest of the Order of the Servants of Mary.

65. *Les carnets du cardinal Alfred Baudrillart* (*26 décembre 1928–12 février 1932*), 584–85.

66. ACS, Ministero dell'Interno, Direzione Generale della Pubblica Sicurezza, Divisione Polizia Politica, b 828, "Mery [sic] Del Val Raffaele."

67. ACS, Ministero dell'Interno, Direzione Generale della Pubblica Sicurezza, Divisione Polizia Politica, b 828, "Mery [sic] Del Val Raffaele," Rome, note of February 27, 1930.

rumors were circulating in the Holy See that he had been assassinated by Professor Giuseppe Bastianelli, the surgeon who had operated on him, and that he was killed by an overdose of chloroform. The same note stated that this suspicion had been communicated to Pius XI and pointed out that a strict discretion had been maintained on the "incident" amongst the entourage of the secretary of state. Despite this, the grave accusation against the surgeon circulated throughout the Holy See. The note added that Professor Milani, director general of health services of the Vatican City, had not denied the rumors but had only shrugged his shoulders.[68] Later, on March 5, a note made reference, for the first time, to the cardinal's dentures.[69] The next day, another note related that some placed the responsibility on Professor Bastianelli, accusing him of negligence—some even accused him of being a morphine addict.[70] Nineteen days later, a new note informed the minister of the interior that the pope wanted an inquest to be held to establish the cause of the cardinal's death, since there were so many rumors spreading inside and outside the Vatican to the effect that he had been "killed in a barbarous manner through the inexpe-

68. ACS, Ministero dell'Interno, Direzione Generale della Pubblica Sicurezza, Divisione Polizia Politica, b 828, "Mery [sic] Del Val Raffaele," Rome, note of February 27, 1930.

69. ACS, Ministero dell'Interno, Direzione Generale della Pubblica Sicurezza, Divisione Polizia Politica, b 828, "Mery [sic] Del Val Raffaele," Rome, note of March 5, 1930.

70. ACS, Ministero dell'Interno, Direzione Generale della Pubblica Sicurezza, Divisione Polizia Politica, b 828, "Mery [sic] Del Val Raffaele," Rome, note of March 6, 1930.

rience and faults of the doctors."[71] Was this inquest held? There is no mention of it in the archives. As for Msgr. Canali, he spread the idea that it was an assassination. A noted dated April 30, 1930, reported the following:

One of our Catholic informants yesterday met Msgr. Canali who was a protégé of the deceased Cardinal Merry del Val and who had a fraternal familiarity with him.

Msgr. Canali, a very frank sort of person who says what he thinks, said this:

"In the case of the death of the current sovereign pontiff, the only Cardinal who had the certain probability of being elected pope was certainly the deceased and lamented Merry del Val. Naturally, this death was not upsetting to someone today in an eminent position in the entourage of Pius XI.

I will never stop shouting that H. E. Merry del Val was assassinated."

As our informant looked at him in astonishment, Msgr. Canali repeated:

"Yes, assassinated. Because the professional qualifications of doctors such as Bastianelli and the others cannot be questioned, we have the right to say that their error was murder, even if it be involuntary.

"These fools of doctors have not yet sent me the bill for the operation, but when they come to collect it, they will hear me out!"

Msgr. Canali answered a question from our informant in this way:

71. ACS, Ministero dell'Interno, Direzione Generale della Pubblica Sicurezza, Divisione Polizia Politica, b 828, "Mery [sic] Del Val Raffaele," Rome, note of March 25, 1930.

"It is true that the brother of the lamented Cardinal Merry del Val wanted to denounce the three fools and crooks; but we would also have had to implicate Professor Milani who enjoys the favor of Msgr. Pizzardo.

"And so everything is covered over by silence and the Bastianellis are out of it. I ask myself, concluded Msgr. Canali, what would have happened, if, by mistake, Professor Bastianelli had killed a person important to the fascists. And I am told that this person still enjoys the confidence of Il Duce!"

And so Msgr. Canali sounded off to one of our Catholic informants.[72]

In addition, a little while after the death of Cardinal Merry del Val, Dr. Ernesto Boni, the anesthesiologist, died. At the beginning of the month of June, an informative note from the political police mentioned that he had not died unexpectedly but that, according to Msgr. Canali and others, he committed suicide.[73]

The last note in the dossier on Rafael Merry del Val, which is in the Archivio Centrale dello Stato, dated August 30, 1933, concluded that the suffocation of the cardinal was caused by his dentures. These were found in the back of his throat—dentures that they had not removed, not having suitable surgical pliers to hand.[74] However,

72. ACS, Ministero dell'Interno, Direzione Generale della Pubblica Sicurezza, Divisione Polizia Politica, b 828, "Mery [sic] Del Val Raffaele", Rome, note of April 13, 1930.

73. ACS, Ministero dell'Interno, Direzione Generale della Pubblica Sicurezza, Divisione Polizia Politica, b 828, "Mery [sic] Del Val Raffaele," Rome, note of June 8, 1930.

74. ACS, Ministero dell'Interno, Direzione Generale della Pubblica Si-

this version, as accepted by the political police, poses a problem and does not stand up under serious investigation. First of all, contemporaries of the cardinal who knew him well, one of whom was his dentist, affirmed that the cardinal did not have dentures, but only had a filled molar.[75] And then, in his testimony for the process of the cardinal's beatification, the surgeon who had operated on him affirmed that this was not the cause of his death and gave a detailed account of the operation, from which is this extract:

There was a discussion with Dr. Milani over which was the best way to administer anesthesia, that is, whether by general anesthetic or injection, as they say, lumbar [local anesthetic]. From the movements that His Eminence made while being examined, we had already observed that the inclined position, necessary for performing it by injection, was not well tolerated, given the condition of the sick stomach and His Eminence's complexion. They also discussed the eventu-

curezza, Divisione Polizia Politica, b 828, "Mery [sic] Del Val Raffaele," Rome, note of August 30, 1933.

75. *Vaticana beatificationis et canonizationis Servi Dei Raphaëlis Card. Merry del Val*, 209–10, testimony of Luigi Nardini, member of the Association of the Sacred Heart, who reported a telephone statement made to him by the Cardinal's dentist: "Per causa del narcotico fu soffocato dalla lingua e non per la dentiera cadutagli nella gola come fu detto e pubblicato perchè non aveva dentiera mobile, ma solo un dente molare piombato, secondo la dichiarazione telefonica del dentista, fatta a me." See also, in the same document, p. 197, the testimony of Enrico Mascioli, adjunct director of the *Musei Lateranensi*, who said, "Fu detto che il Servo di Dio fosse morte per soffocamento a causa della dentiera ma io so con sicurezza che il Servo di Dio non aveva affatto una dentiera, ma aveva solamente qualche capsula d'oro."

alities of the lack of success of the anesthesia by the lumbar method. They decided in favor of general anesthetic using ether, which was administered by Dr. Boni, the specialist in this matter. Present besides the two assistants [Drs. Bardellini and Boni], were Dr. Milani and Mother Esther, who handed the instruments.

Once the patient had reached the expected stage of anesthesia, I proceeded with the operation. After a few minutes, while I was in the middle of removing the appendix, I saw that the wound was not bleeding. I immediately stopped; I turned around and I saw that His Eminence was not breathing. I immediately performed a tracheotomy because once we started artificial respiration, we found that air was not passing well through the natural airways. The respiration continued for about one hour before being abandoned, given its lack of success.

Question: To what factor could you attribute this unexpected phenomenon?

Response: I was not in the position to establish which factor or factors caused this event in the case in question. The doctor and the surgeon have known for a long time and always with great precision that the arrest of the cardiac function and of respiration could happen instantaneously during operations, even minor ones, and the cause cannot be established.

... I absolutely exclude that he was suffocated by a foreign body, that is, by his dentures. I can add nothing.[76]

As for the religious sister who was present during the operation, Sr. Esther Di Giusto, she stated, "The Servant of

76. *Vaticana beatificationis et canonizationis Servi Dei Raphaëlis Card. Merry del Val* (1957), 242, testimony of Professor Dr. Guiseppe Bastianelli.

God had a blackout; it was a definite case of cardiac arrest."[77] Nevertheless, taken as a whole, her testimony on the surgical intervention does not contradict that of Professor Bastianelli.[78]

The exact cause of the death of Cardinal Merry del Val remains an enigma on which the accessible documentation does not provide any clarity. The hypothesis of murder seems unlikely. Who would want to kill him, and why? Who would have benefited? Also, it would have been difficult to assassinate the cardinal because there were numerous people around him at the time of the operation. Furthermore, the rumors about murder seem to come from Msgr. Canali, whose testimony, according to the archives, does not appear to be completely reliable. The hypothesis of a medical problem is much more likely. For example, the possibility of an allergic reaction to the particular anesthetic should considered.

For the time being, the exact cause of death of the cardinal is not known, and the archives do not allow for further conclusions. To know more, there would have to be an autopsy.

77. *Vaticana beatificationis et canonizationis Servi Dei Raphaëlis Card. Merry del Val*, 250, testimony of Sr. Esther Di Giusto.

78. *Vaticana beatificationis et canonizationis Servi Dei Raphaëlis Card. Merry del Val*, 248–50.

CONCLUSION

CARDINAL Rafael Merry del Val had a dazzling and exceptional career. If we consider only his most important appointments: he was private supernumerary chamberlain—thus *Monsignore*—at twenty-one years of age, private participant chamberlain at twenty-six, apostolic delegate to Canada at thirty-one, president of the Academy of Ecclesiastical Nobles and archbishop at thirty-four, secretary of state and cardinal at thirty-eight, archpriest of St. Peter's Basilica and prefect of the Fabric of St. Peter at forty-eight, secretary of the Holy Office at forty-nine. How can this brilliant career be explained?

First among the reasons that should be considered is the particular affection Leo XIII had for him. This was the pope who gave him his first assignments and his first honors, without the young man having sought them— quite the opposite. Rafael Merry del Val aspired to only one thing: to return to England and devote himself to the conversion of the Anglicans. The archives prove it without doubt. So, for example, when he learned that he had been named secret participant chamberlain, the young priest asked Leo XIII to take back his decision and to let him leave for England. This was in vain.[1] Earlier, before the rumors flowed through Rome on the subject of his appointment, he had written to a religious sister, "Nothing of this type [of position] could be more contrary to my aspirations; I think that Our Lord would give me the grace to bring me back to this life rather than inflict such a thing on me."[2] Later, on his return from Canada, he hoped that the discontent of those who were opposed to his politics and who were trying to destroy his reputation with the pope and his superiors would enable him to leave the Vatican and consecrate himself to the ministry of souls. Once again, this was in vain.[3]

One other element that explains Rafael Merry del Val's ascent through the Curia, even though its importance cannot be exactly measured, is the consideration that Leo XIII had for the cardinal's father and the presence of the latter in Rome as an ambassador close to the Holy See from 1893 to 1901. Leo XIII so esteemed this man that he conferred upon him the rank of [Knight of the] Grand Cross of the Order of Pius IX, then made him a member of the Order of Christ.[4] Upon each new honor given to his son, the ambassador wrote to Cardinal Rampolla to

1. Cenci, *Il cardinale Raffaele Merry del Val*, 49–50.

2. Cited by Cenci, *Il cardinale Raffaele Merry del Val*, 50.

3. Pontificio Colegio Español de San José, Archivo Merry del Val (PCESJ, AMDV), copy of a letter—"Concordat cum originali"—from Rafael Merry del Val to a certain Fr. Lacoste, Vatican, October 7, 1897.

4. Cenci, *Il cardinale Raffaele Merry del Val*, 7.

ask him to give his thanks to Leo XIII.[5] It was pure protocol and politeness, but certainly not without psychological effect on the aged pontiff.

To understand the career of Rafael Merry del Val, it is necessary to emphasize his membership in the nobility, of great importance at that time, as well as his aptitudes, his competences, and his personal qualities, among which must be noted his meticulous education and his good manners, his sociability, and his linguistic, diplomatic, and geopolitical knowledge, as well as his formation in philosophy, theology, and law.

The path of Rafael Merry del Val can also be explained by his devotion toward the papacy. He was not a party man. Pius X, as we have emphasized, said that one of the reasons he chose him was that he did not compromise.[6] His reputation for holiness should also be taken into consideration. For, as Pius X explicitly told a cardinal,[7] it did play a part in his appointment as secretary of state.

Finally, the combination of circumstances should not be neglected. What would the life of Rafael Merry del Val have been like if he had not been received in an audience with Leo XIII upon returning to the Scottish College?

5. For example: Archivio Segreto Vaticano (ASV), Segreteria di Stato, Spogli di Cardinali e Officiali di Curia, Rafael Merry del Val, busta 3, fol. 120, letter from Cardinal Mariano Rampolla to Rafael Merry del Val (senior), Rome, June 16, 1887; fol. 148, letter from Cardinal Mariano Rampolla del Tindaro, written by Msgr. Giacomo della Chiesa, to Rafael Merry del Val (senior), Rome, January 12, 1892.

6. Cenci, *Il cardinale Raffaele Merry del Val*, 138.

7. Cenci, *Il cardinale Raffaele Merry del Val*, 138.

What would his life have been like if Msgr. Volpini had not died just before the conclave?

It is the ensemble of these factors that must be considered to understand the life of Rafael Merry del Val.

Bibliography

Archival Sources

Archives du Ministère des Affaires Étrangères—La Courneuve
Archivio Centrale dello Stato
Archivio della basilica di Santa Prassede
Archivio della Congregazione delle Cause dei Santi
Archivio della Congregazione per la Dottrina della Fede
Archivio della Fabbrica di San Pietro
Archivio della Pia Associazione del Sacro Cuore di Gesù in
    Trastevere
Archivio della Pontificia Accademia Ecclesiastica
Archivio della Sacra Congregazione degli Affari Ecclesiastici
    Straordinari
Archivio Segreto Vaticano
Archivio Storico di Propaganda Fide
Archivo de la Postulación (Pontificio Colegio Español de San José)
Archivo del Pontificio Colegio Español de San José
Archivo General de los Operarios Diocesanos
Archivo Histórico de la Embajada de España ante la Santa Sede
KADOC-KU Leuven, Documentatie- en Onderzoekscentrum
    voor Religie, Cultuur en Samenleving, Archives du Collège
    Saint-Michel (Bruxelles)

Pontifical Beda College Archives

Ushaw College Library, Merry del Val papers; see *Catalogue of the Merry del Val Papers* (Durham, U.K.: University of Durham, 2012)

Print Sources

Abadie, Célestin. *Menée du Cardinal Merry del Val faisant expulser d'Italie un Français: Protestation de l'abbé Célestin Abadie*. Paris: Impr. de la Bourse de Commerce, 1912.

Acta Apostolicae Sedis. Commentarium officiale. Rome: Typis Polyglottis Vaticanis.

Acta Sanctae Sedis. Rome: Typographia Polyglotta.

Annuario Pontificio. Rome: Tipografia Poliglotta Vaticana.

Assisi al Cardinale Merry del Val, Giorno di S. Francesco 1926-IV ottobre-1933. Rome: Tipografia Romana "Buona Stampa," 1934.

Forti, Francesco. *Nel XXV anno della consacrazione episcopale di Sua Eminenza Reverendissima il signor cardinale Raffaele Merry del Val fervidissimi voti al cielo innalza in poetici accenti Mons. Francesco Forti da oltre quattro lustri ammiratore assiduo delle altissime doti che mirabilmente illustrano l'insigne porporato e ai tanti plausi unisce il suo rispettoso omaggio che con somma venerazione e riconoscenza giubilando offre*. Rome: Tipografica Vaticana, 1925.

Gerarchia Cattolica. Rome: Tipografia Vaticana.

Hommage à Monseigneur Raphaël Merry del Val, délégué apostolique au Canada: Souvenir de la visite de Son Excellence à Valleyfield, 21, 22 et 23 avril 1897. Valleyfield: E. H. Solis, 1897.

Iasoni, Erminio. *Come ho visto il cardinale Raffaele Merry del Val*. Rome: Officina Tipografica Romana "Buona Stampa," 1930.

Il convento francescano di Fontecolombo (Rieti) in memoria del cardinale Raffaele Merry del Val: Venerdì 24 ottobre 1930; Festa

dell'arcangelo san Raffaele. Rome: Industria Tipografica
Romana, 1930.

Jeremich, Giovanni. *Riese Veneto terra natale del papa Pio X a
perenne e devoto ricordo del cardinale Raffaele Merry del Val:
Discorso commemorativo di Sua Ecc. Rev.ma Monsignor Giovanni
Jeremich*. Venice: Libreria Emiliana Editrice, 1933.

Landry, Philippe. *Observations sur la nomination d'un délégué
apostolique au Canada*. Rome[?], 1897.

McLeod, Pierre. *Mémoire à son Excellence Mgr Merry del Val, délégué
apostolique au Canada*. S.l., s.d.

*Nella Patriarcale Basilica di San Pietro in Vaticano: Inaugurazione
della nuova tomba e del monumento-ricordo del cardinale
Raffaele Merry del Val alla presenza di Sua Eminenza Revma il
signor Cardinale Eugenio Pacelli, Segretario di Stato di S. Santità,
Arciprete della Basilica Vaticana. 11 luglio 1931*. Tipografia
Poliglotta Vaticana, 1931.

*Recuerdo del homenaje de veneración cariño que al Emmo. y Rvdmo.
Sr. Cardenal Rafael Merry del Val: Dedicó con la fausta ocasión
del XXV aniversario de su consagración episcopal el Pontificio
Colegio Español de San José*. Rome: Pontificio Colegio Español
de San José, 1925[?].

Ruffini, Ernesto. *Nel primo anniversario della morte del cardinale
Raffaele Merry del Val: Discorso commemorativo tenuto nella
basilica di S. Prassede da sua Eccellenza Revma Monsignor
Ernesto Ruffini Segretario della Sacra Congregazione dei Seminari
e delle Università degli studi*. Tipografia Poliglotta Vaticana,
1931.

Sacra Rituum Congregatio. Sectio Historica. *Romana
beatificationis et canonizationis Servi Dei Pii Papae X: Disquisitio
circa quasdam obiectiones modum agendi servi dei respicientes
in modernismi debellatione una cum Summario Additionali
ex Officio Compilato*. Civitate Vaticana: Typis Polyglottis
Vaticanis, 1950.

Documents on the Process of Beatification

*Beatificazione e canonizzazione del servo di Dio il cardinale Raffaele
  Merry del Val, Segretario di Stato del beato Pio X: Articoli per il
  processo ordinario informativo.* Tipografia Poliglotta Vaticana,
  1952.

*Relazione sul processo di beatificazione e canonizzazione del servo di
  Dio Raffaele cardinale Merry del Val nel Vicariato per la Città del
  Vaticano.* Unpublished , n.d.

Cocchetti, Horatius. *Copia Publica.* 1956. 5 vols. manuscripts:

> *Copia Publica transumpti Processus Ordinaria auctoritate
>   in Vicariatu Civitatis Vaticanae constructi super Cultu
>   numquam praestito Servo Dei Raphaëli Card. Merry del Val
>   Secretario Status S. Pii Papae X.* Vol. unic., f 1–64.

> *Copia Publica transumpti Processus Ordinaria auctoritate
>   in Vicariatu Civitatis Vaticanae constructi super fama
>   sanctitatis vitae, virtutum et miraculorum Servi Dei Raphaëlis
>   Card. Merry del Val Secretarii Status S. Pii Papae X.* Vol. 1,
>   f 1–277; vol. 2, f 278–648 ; vol. 3, f 649–968.

> *Copia Publica transumptor: Processuum Rogat. in Curiis Matriten,
>   Limana, Westmonasterien, Birminghamien, Hispalen,
>   et in Vicariatu ap. Maroquien constructorum super fama
>   sanctitatis vitae, virtutum et miraculorum Servi Dei Raphaëlis
>   Card. Merry del Val Secretarii Status S. Pii Papae X.* Vol.
>   unic., f 1–226.

Sacra Rituum Congregatione. Cardinali Clemente Micara,
  Ponente. (Sub secreto.) *Romana beatificationis et
  canonizationis servi dei Raphaëlis Merry del Val S. R. E.
  Cardinalis: Summarium ex officio super scriptis.* Typis
  Polyglottis Vaticanis, 1956.

*Romana beatificationis et canonizationis Servi Dei Raphaëlis Card.
  Merry del Val Secretarii Status Sancti Pii Papae X. Informatio—
  Tabella testium—Summarium litterae postulatoriae super causae*

introductione et summarium ex officio super scriptis. Rome: Typis Polyglottis Vaticanis, 1957:

    Romana beatificationis et canonizationis Servi Dei Raphaëlis Card. Merry del Val Secretarii Status Sancti Pii Papae X: Informatio super dubio An signanda sit Commissio introductionis causae in casu et ad effectum de quo agitur. Tabella et index testium. 1957.

    Vaticana beatificationis et canonizationis Servi Dei Raphaëlis Card. Merry del Val Secretarii Status Sancti Pii Papae X: Summarium super dubio An signanda sit Commissio introductionis Causae in casu et ad effectum de quo agitur. 1957.

    Romana beatificationis et canonizationis Servi Dei Raphaëlis Card. Merry del Val Secretarii Status Sancti Pii Papae X: Litterae postulatoriae pro impetranda signatura commissionis introductionis causae. 1957.

Sacra Rituum Congregatione. *Romana beatificationis et canonizationis Servi Dei Raphaëlis Card. Merry del Val. Secretarii Status Sancti Pii Papae X: Animadversiones promotoris generalis fidei. Super dubio an signanda sit commissio introductionis causae in casu et ad effectum de quo agitur.* Typis Polyglottis Vaticanis, 1959.

Romana beatificationis et canonizationis Servi Dei Raphaëlis Merry del Val Cardinalis (1865–1930): Summarium Additivum; Super dubio An constet de virtutibus theologalibus Fide, Spe, Caritate tum in Deum tum in proximum, necnon de cardinalibus Prudentia, Iustitia, Fortitudine, Temperantia earumque adnexis, in gradu heroico et ad effectum de quo agitur. Rome, 1995.

Writings of Cardinal Rafael Merry del Val

Fairlie, Paula, ed. *Let God Act: Selections from the Spiritual Writings of Cardinal Rafael Merry del Val*. Worcester: Legion of Merry del Val, 1974.

Merry del Val, Rafael. "St. Aloysius." *Ushaw Magazine* (June 1891), 89–94.

———. *Una risposta al sermone pronunciato a Roma il 15 novembre 1896 da F. B. Oxenham*. Rome: Catholic Truth Society, 1897.

———. *The Truth of Papal Claims: A Reply to "The Validity of Papal Claims" by F. Nutcombe Oxenham, D.D. English Chaplain in Rome*. London: Sands; St. Louis: B. Herder, 1904.

———. *Regolamento per la redazione ed amministrazione del Bollettino Ufficiale "Acta Apostolicae Sedis."* (Rome: 1910[?]).

———. "A proposito delle ordinazioni anglicane: Un documento inedito." *La Civiltà Cattolica*, quaderno 1489, year 63, vol. 3 (July 6, 1912): 79–106.

———. *Discorso di Sua Eminenza Revma Il Cardinale R. Merry del Val per la solenne inaugurazione del monumento al papa Pio X nella patriarcale basilica Vaticana alla presenza di Sua Santità Pio XI e del Sacro Collegio il 28 giugno 1923*. Rome: Tipografia Poliglotta Vaticana, 1923.

———. *Notes de direction*. Paris: Éditions du Cerf, 1937.

———. *Spiritual Directions*. London: Burns Oates, and Washbourne, 1937.

———. *Worte der Führung*. Luzern: Räber, 1938.

———. *Notas de direccion*. Brasil: Libreria Editorial Santa Catalina, 1941.

———. *Memorias del Papa Pío X*. Madrid: Soc. Atenas, 1946.

———. *Pío X: Impressioni e Ricordi*. Padua: Il Messaggero di S. Antonio, 1949.

———. *Memories of Pope Pius X*. Westminster, Md.: Newman Press, 1951.

———. *Pie X: Impressions et souvenirs*. Saint-Maurice: Éditions de l'oeuvre de St-Augustin, 1951.

———. *Pius X: Erinnerungen und Eindrücke*. Basel: Thomas Morus Verl., 1951.

———. *Pensieri ascetici del servo di Dio cardinale Raffaele Merry del Val Segretario di Stato di San Pio X*. Rome: Postulazione presso il Pontificio Collegio Spagnolo, 1953.

———. *Pensamientos asceticos del siervo de Dios*. 2nd ed. Madrid: Edic. Paulinas, [1959].

———. *Écrits spirituels*. S.l.: Le vrai visage de l'Église, 1993 (outside trade).

———. *El Papa San Pío X: Memorias*. Buenos Aires: Ediciones Fundación San Pío X, 2006.

———. *San Pio X: Un santo che ho conosciuto da vicino*. Verona: Fede and cultura, 2012.

Weber, Francis J., ed. *The Spiritual Diary of Raphael Cardinal Merry del Val*. New York: Exposition Press, 1964.

Works on Cardinal Rafael Merry del Val

Almandoz, Norberto. "El Cardenal Merry del Val, compositor de música." *ABC de Sevilla* (March 21, 1956): 5.

Anderson, Robin. "Mémorial: Le Cardinal Merry del Val: Secrétaire d'État de saint Pie X." *Permanences* (June–July 1966): 57–61.

———. "Il cardinale Merry del Val." *Tabor: Rivista di vita spirituale*, no. 3–4 (March–April 1969): 91–94.

Bazin, René. "Le cardinal Merry del Val." *Revue des Deux Mondes* (June 15, 1931): 288–303.

Berto, Victor-Alain. "À la mémoire du serviteur de Dieu le Cardinal Raphaël Merry del Val." *La Pensée catholique*, no. 26 (3rd trimester, 1953): 42–46.

Buehrle, Marie Cecilia. *Rafael cardinal Merry del Val*. Milwaukee:
Bruce, 1957.

Canestri, Alberto. *Un missionario in porpora: S. Em. il cardinale
Merry del Val*. Rome: Unione missionaria del clero in Italia,
1934.

Cárcel Ortí, Vincente. "Instrucciones de Merry del Val a Vico en
1907 y relación final del Nuncio en 1912." *Revista española de
derecho canónico* 49, no. 133 (1992): 567–605.

———. "Intervención del Cardenal Merry del Val en los
nombramientos de Obispos españoles (1903–1914)."
Archivum Historiae Pontificiae 32 (1994): 253–91.

Carli, Ferruccio. *Il cardinale Merry del Val*. Rome: Extract of "La
vita italiana," 1934.

Carroll-Abbing, John Patrick (Giovanni Patrizio). *Cardinal Merry
del Val*. London: Catholic Truth Society, 1937.

———. *Serviro Dio per Amore: Il Card. Merry del Val ed i giovani*.
Città del Vaticano: Tipografia Poliglotta Vaticana, 1973.

———. *Cardinale Merry del Val: Il Rinnovamento in Cristo*. Città
del Vaticano: Tipografia Poliglotta Vaticana, 1974.

Cenci, Pio. *Il cardinale Raffaele Merry del Val*. Rome and Turin:
L.I.C.E. and Roberto Berruti, 1933.

Chimenton, Costante. *Nel V. anniversario dalla morte di Sua
Eminenza il cardinale Raffaele Merry del Val, Segretario di Stato
di Pio X*. Treviso: Tip. Ep. Trevigiana, 1935.

Claar, Maximilian. "Das Staatssekretariat Merry del Val (1903–
1914)." *Zeitschrift für Politik* 20 (1931): 30–42.

Dal-Gal, Girolamo. *Il Cardinale Raffaele Merry de Val: Segretario di
Stato del Beato Pio X*. Rome: Edizioni Paoline, 1953.

———. *El Cardenal Rafael Merry del Val: Secretario de estado de
San Pio X, Papa*. Madrid: Editorial Sapientia, 1954.

———. *Le cardinal Merry del Val*. Translation and preface by
Robert Havard de La Montagne. Paris: Nouvelles Éditions
Latines, 1955.

————. *The Spiritual Life of Cardinal Merry del Val*. New York: Benziger Brothers, 1959.

Dalla Torre, Giuseppe. *Il card. Raffaele Merry del Val: Commemorazione letta nell'Aula Magna della cancelleria apostolica il giorno 6 aprile 1930*. Milan: Soc. ed. Vita e pensiero, 1930.

————. *The Cardinal of Charity. Memorial Discourse on the Work and Virtues of the Late Cardinal Raphael Merry del Val*. New York: Paulist Press, 1932.

Dalpiaz, Vigilio. *Attraverso una porpora: Il cardinale Merry del Val*. Turin: L.I.C.E., Roberto Berruti, 1935.

————. *Il Cardinale Raffaele Merry del Val*. Turin: L.I.C.E.–R. Berruti e C. Torino (Fiori di Cielo, 109), 1935.

————. *Cardinal Merry del Val*. London: Burns, Oats and Washbourne, 1937.

D'Angelantonio, Cesare. "Il monumento a San Pio X: Lo scultore Pier Enrico Astorri e il Cardinale Merry del Val." *Strena dei Romanisti* (1968): 113–19.

De Filippis, Orietta. "Rafael Merry del Val: Il cardinale che amò Trastevere." *Lazio, ieri e oggi*, no. 9 (September 2013): 274–77.

de Viñayo, Cándido. *Senda luminosa: Vida del cardenal Merry del Val*. Zalla: Ed. Paulinas (Lo Hijos de la luz, 2), 1959.

Dick, John A. "Cardinal Merry del Val and the Malines Conversations." *Ephemerides Theologicae Lovanienses: Louvain Journal of Theology and Canon Law* 62 (1986): 333–55.

Facchinetti, Vittorino. "L'anima francescana del Cardinale Merry del Val." *Frate Francesco: Rivista di cultura francescana* 6, no. 4 (July–August 1933): 285–89.

Fèvre, Justin. *S. Em. le Cardinal Merry del Val, Secrétaire d'État de S. S. Pie X*. Paris: Arthur Savaète, 1904.

Figueroa Ortega, Rafael. *Una gloria de la Iglesia: El Cardenal Rafael Merry del Val*. Puebla, México: La Enseñanza, 1937.

Flores de Lemus, Isabel. *El fulgor de una purpura: El Cardenal*

Rafael Merry del Val. Madrid: Editorial El Perpetuo Socorro, 1956.

Forbes, Frances Alice. *Rafael, Cardinal Merry del Val: A Character Sketch*. London, New York, and Toronto: Longmans, Green, 1932.

Giacchi, Orio. "Il cardinale Raffaele Merry del Val." *Vita e Pensiero*," 19, vol. 24, new series, fasc. 5 (May 1933): 288–95.

Gilley, Sheridan. "Merry del Val, Rafael María José Pedro Francisco Borja Domingo Gerardo de la Santísma Trinidad." *Oxford Dictionary of National Biography*. 37:925–29.

González Chaves, Alberto José. *Rafael Merry del Val*. Madrid: San Pablo, 2004.

———. "El cardenal Rafael Merry del Val: A 76 años de su muerte." *Humanitas* 11, no. 41 (Summer 2006): 116–29.

Goulmy, Paul J. L. M. *Paus Pius X en zijn staatssecretaris Kardinaal Merry del Val: Hun beleid en hunne daden, tegenover hunne tallooze vijanden verdedigd*. Druten: De Maas en Waler, 1911.

Holmes, J. Derek. "Cardinal Raphael Merry del Val: An Uncompromising Ultramontane: Gleanings from His Correspondence with England." *Catholic Historical Review*, no. 60 (1974): 55–64.

Javierre, José María. *La diplomacia de Merry del Val en los grandes estados*. Academic thesis under the supervision of the professor Luis Sala Balust. Universidad Pontificia de Salamanca, [1960 ?]. http://koha.upsa.es/cgi-bin/koha/opac-detail.pl?biblionumber=157405#.

———. *Merry del Val*. Barcelona: Juan Flors, 1961.

Lease, Gary. "Merry del Val and Tyrrell: A Modernist Struggle." *Downside Review* 102, no. 347 (April 1984): 133–56.

LeBlanc, Jean. "Merry del Val, Rafael, 1865–1930." *Dictionnaire biographique des évêques catholiques du Canada: Les diocèses catholiques canadiens des Églises latine et orientales et leurs évêques; Repères chronologiques et biographiques 1658–2002*. Ottawa: Wilson and Lafleur, 2002 : 242–245.

Lefebvre, Ch. "Merry Del Val (Raphaël)." *Catholicisme: Hier Aujourd'hui Demain*. Vol. 8. Paris: Letouzey et Ané, 1979.

Llaquet de Entrambasaguas, José Luis. "La diplomacia del Secretario de Estabo de la Santa Sede Merry del Val respecto al Estado Español (1903–1914)." *Revista General de Derecho Canónico y Eclesiástico del Estado*, no. 41 (2016): 1–32.

Miranda, Salvador. *Merry del Val y Zulueta, Rafael*. http://www2.fiu.edu/~mirandas/cardinals.htm.

Mitchell, Hary. "La Grande âme du Secrétaire d'État du Bienheureux Pie X." *La Pensée catholique*, no. 28 (4th trimester 1953): 60–69.

———. *Le cardinal R. Merry del Val: Secrétaire d'État de Saint Pie X*. Paris: Paris-Livres, 1956.

Muñoz Urbano, José María. "El cardenal Secretario de Estado Rafael Merry del Val y su proceso de beatificación: Historia de su causa; Problemas, investigaciones de archivos y documentación inédita." Ph.D. diss. Rome: Pontificia Università Gregoriana, 2008.

Murphy, Harriet, ed. *The Spiritual Writings of Raphael Cardinal Merry del Val*. Leominster: Gracewing, 2009.

Nieva, Soto J. *El Cardenal Rafael Merry del Val y la Cuestión Modernista*. Thesis for the licence in ecclesiastical history, Rome: Pontificia Università Gregoriana, 2001.

Olgiati, Francesco. "Il cardinale Merry del Val e la devozione al Sacro Cuore." *Rivista del Clero Italiano*, year 14, fasc. 6 (June 1933): 347–49.

Oswald, Josef. *Die Außenminister der Päpste: Raffaele Merry del Val* [Manuskript zur Sendung im Bayerischen Rundfunk am 4. März 1962 mit dem. Titel "Katholische Welt"]. Munich, 1962.

Pérez-Caballero y Ferrer, Juan. *La Secretaría de Estado de Su Santidad y el Cardenal Merry del Val*. Madrid, 1903 : 709–730.

Quinn, Mary Bernetta. *Give Me Souls: A Life of Rafael Merry del Val*. Westminster, Md.: Newman Press, 1958.

Raurell, F. "Un cardinale e tre conclave: Merry del Val."
Laurentianum 50, no. 3 (2009): 283–312.

Roland-Gosselin, Dominique. *Un grand prélat souvent méconnu.
Le cardinal Merry del Val.* Unpublished, s.l., s.d. (1952 ?).

———. "Le Cardinal Merry del Val: Les premières années
de son sacerdoce; Les ordinations anglicanes." *La Pensée
catholique,* no. 44 (4th trimester 1956): 31–43.

Romanato, Gianpaolo. "Un aristocrate espagnol aux côtés de
Pie X." *30 Giorni* (April 2006), http://www.30giorni.it.

———. "A 80 años de la muerte del Cardenal Rafael Merry
del Val." *Humanitas,* year 15, no. 58 (2010): 339–43.

Roy-Lysencourt, Philippe. "Le parcours curial du cardinal Rafael
Merry del Val." *Mélanges de l'École française de Rome—Italie
et Méditerranée modernes et contemporaines (MEFRIM)*
[online], 128–1 (2016). Published online January 27, 2016,
http://mefrim.revues.org/2415.

———. "Rafael Merry del Val: Le secrétaire d'État oublié."
L'Homme Nouveau, no. 1623 (October 8, 2016): 17–18.

———. "Une amitié surnaturelle: Pie X et son secrétaire d'État."
L'Homme Nouveau, no. 1623 (Octobre 8, 2016): 18.

———. "Les grands traits de la spiritualité du cardinal Rafael
Merry del Val." *L'Homme Nouveau,* no. 1623 (October 8, 2016):
19–20.

———. *Le cardinal Rafael Merry del Val (1865–1930): Aperçu
biographique.* Strasbourg: Institut d'Étude du Christianisme,
Études 1, 2016.

———. *Le cardinal Rafael Merry del Val (1865–1930).* Strasbourg:
Institut d'Étude du Christianisme, Les conférences de
l'Institut d'Étude du Christianisme 1, 2016. CD audio,
67 min.

———. "Mgr Merry del Val et la réforme des études de
l'Académie des Nobles ecclésiastiques" (1900). In *Le Saint-
Siège, les Églises et l'Europe à l'époque contemporaine: Mélanges*

offerts à Jean-Dominique Durand. Rome: Edizioni Studium, 2018.

Russell, Charles. "Cardinal Raphael Merry del Val: Papal Secretary of State." *Irish Monthly* (April 1904): 192–97.

Valderrama Abenza, Juan Carlos. "Merry Del Val Zulueta-Wilcox, Rafael." In *Diccionario crítico de Juristas Españoles, Portugueses y Latinoamericanos (Hispánicos, Brasileños, Quebequenses y restantes francófonos)*, ed. Manuel J. Peláez, vol. 3, part 4, 368–70. Zaragoza, Barcelona: Manuel J. Peláez, 2012.

———. "Merry Del Val Zulueta-Wilcox, Rafael." In *Diccionario de Canonistas y Eclesiasticistas europeos y americanos*, ed. Manuel J. Peláez, 309–11. Saarbrücken: Editorial Académica Española, AV Akademikerverlag, 2012.

Visani, Alessandro. "La misteriosa morte del cardinale Merry del Val nelle carte della polizia politica fascista." *Giornale di storia* 7 (2011), www.giornaledistoria.net.

von Hettlingen, Viktor. *Raphael Kardinal Merry del Val: Ein Lebensbild*. Einsiedeln and Cologne: Benziger, 1937.

Wolff, Joachim. *Kardinal Merry del Val*. Breslau: Franke, 1939.

Zambarbieri, Annibale. "Merry del Val, Rafael." *Dizionario Biografico degli Italiani*. Vol. 73. 2009.

Index

Cardinal Rafael Merry del Val: A Brief Biography was designed in Filosofia with Mr Eaves and Abril Fatface display types and composed by Kachergis Book Design of Pittsboro, North Carolina.